BIRTHPLACE OF AN ARMY

A Study of the Valley Forge Encampment

By John B. B. Trussell, Jr.

Commonwealth of Pennsylvania

PENNSYLVANIA HISTORICAL AND MUSEUM COMMISSION

Harrisburg, 1976

Contents

Introduction

THE winter encampment at Valley Forge, spanning the six months from December 19, 1777, to June 19, 1778, marked as it was by cold weather, recurrent starvation, rampant disease, and near nakedness, has come to be viewed as symbolizing the suffering—and the dogged determination through which that suffering was overcome—of the Continental soldier.

Certainly, there was suffering in plenty, and certainly it was endured and overcome. However, it is no detraction from the credit which is due to the men who lived through the winter at Valley Forge to point out that in terms neither of the severity of the weather nor the shortages of supplies was the winter of 1777-1778 the worst that the American troops survived during the American Revolution.

Yet the winter at Valley Forge was unique in a way which was of both immediate and lasting significance. The fact is that, for the first time since the war began, there existed in combination an adequate concentration of forces, a sufficient period of time uninterrupted by the need to respond to enemy interference, and an individual who had the ability, was granted the authority, and commanded the necessary confidence to permit a comprehensive training, reorganization, and standardization program to be carried out.

It would be unjust and inaccurate to characterize the force which straggled in to Valley Forge on December 19, 1777, as little more than an armed rabble. It had a company, regimental, and brigade structure, but the organizational components varied widely, not merely in manning levels but in theoretical organizational composition as well. It had a hierarchy of command, but its officers tended to have only sparse knowledge of their duties and narrowly limited conceptions of their responsibilities. It was governed by a body of military law, but it equated discipline almost exclusively with punishment. Some of its components had been exposed to fragmentary training, but in accordance with differing theories and doctrines; further, the rapid turn-over in personnel, due to expiration of short-term enlistments, casualties, desertions, and the replacement of veterans by raw recruits, had seriously diluted such levels of training as had existed.

The force which left the encampment the following June, by contrast, had undergone a fundamental change. Legally speaking, of course, the Continental Army was born of a resolution by the Second Continental Congress on June 14, 1775. As an organized, cohesive, proficient force, however—as an army in the full sense of the word— it came into being in the snow and mud of Valley Forge.

It is this fact, as well as the persistence and the dedication shown in surmounting the daily misery and hardship, which makes Valley Forge uniquely important in the history of the ultimate victory which was won and of the new nation which was brought into being.

ACKNOWLEDGMENT

A word of appreciation is in order to those who made the publicacation of this study possible, first to the members of the Pennsylvania Historical and Museum Commission, who approved its publication, and to its Executive Director, Mr. William J. Wewer; and also to Mr. Harry E. Whipkey, Director of the Bureau of Archives and History; Mr. William A. Hunter, Chief of the Division of History, who supervised its preparation; and Mr. Harold L. Myers, Associate Historian, who handled publication.

Schematic of the Valley Forge Encampment 1777~177

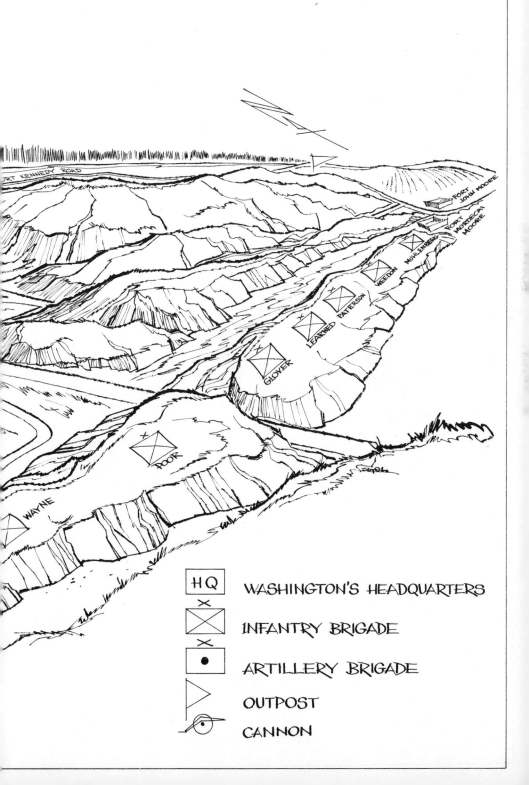

FORT KENNEDY ROAD

FORT JOHN MOORE

FORT MORDECAI MOORE

MUHLENBERG

WEEDON

PATERSON

LEARNED

GLOVER

POOR

WAYNE

HQ	WASHINGTON'S HEADQUARTERS
⊠	INFANTRY BRIGADE
▣	ARTILLERY BRIGADE
▷	OUTPOST
⊙	CANNON

George Washington, by Charles Willson Peale

I

The Road To Mount Joy

VALLEY FORGE: THE PLACE

THE area in which the American army was encamped during the winter of 1777-1778 is contained within a rough triangle of some two thousand acres. Bounded on the north for nearly three miles by the Schuylkill River, its western edge extends along Valley Creek for about a mile and a half, and its southeastern limits stretch for three and a quarter miles along a low ridge which slopes off gently toward Trout Creek on the east. Valley Creek twists northward through a steep gorge for almost a mile, then through leveling ground until it empties into the Schuylkill about a half mile beyond. The eastern wall of the gorge is formed by a ridge, extending northward from Mount Joy (which rises to a height of more than four hundred feet) for a half mile along a saddle to a somewhat lower hill, then veering northeast along another saddle to a 350-foot hill. The western wall of the gorge is formed by the eastern end of a ridge crowned by Mount Misery (like Mount Joy, named decades before the American Revolution), topping Mount Joy by a good 150 feet. On the north, the level ground drops off fairly abruptly to the river, in some sections so sharply as to form steep bluffs.

By 1777, a few buildings—dwellings and workshops—had clustered around the mouth of Valley Creek, and the scattered houses of the farmers, largely Quakers,[1] who cultivated the cleared fields to the east, west, and south, dotted the countryside. The hills and the ridges from which they rose, however, were still covered by virgin forest.

Originally, the tract containing the future encampment was part of the seventy-eight hundred-acre "Manor of Mount Joy," which, on October 24, 1701, William Penn granted to his daughter, Letitia, in return for an annual rent of one beaver skin. Over the years, Letitia and her husband, William Aubrey, sold portions of the manor, the last remaining parcel, of 175 acres, being disposed of on July 10, 1730. After changing hands several times, this parcel came into the joint possession, on December 13, 1742, of Stephen Evans, Daniel Walker, and Joseph Williams. Having formed a partnership, these three soon afterwards developed the "Mount Joy Forge," which later came to be known more commonly as the "Valley Forge."[2]

1

The name may be misleading. What it described was not a simple blacksmith shop but a complete ironworks: it included a bloomery, a finery, a chafery, and a slitting mill; it converted pig iron into billets and cast iron into wrought iron, drew iron billets into bars, and manufactured finished metal products.

The wooded hills provided a source of charcoal, and Valley Creek supplied ample water power. Indeed, at some time between 1751 and 1757 the two remaining partners (Daniel Walker seems to have sold his one-third interest in 1751) added a sawmill. By the latter year—1757—the entire property had been purchased by John Potts, a prominent Quaker ironmaster. In 1758 or 1759, partly to meet the needs of the workers at the forge and partly to provide materials for wider sale, he expanded his activity by erecting a gristmill.[3] Such an operation, in fact, required a considerable labor force, not only to work the iron but also to cut and haul the wood and charcoal. Since transportation was slow and difficult, most of the food for the workers had to be obtained from nearby sources. Thus Valley Forge, like similar establishments throughout Pennsylvania, was a nucleus of an essentially self-sustaining economic unit.[4] As at other iron forges, many of the Valley Forge workers, both skilled and unskilled, were Negroes— some of them slaves, some freemen.[5]

By 1767, the "Mount Joy Forge" was being operated by the firm of Potts, Hackley & Potts, which consisted of John Potts's sons, Joseph and David, and their cousin, Thomas Hackley; but on May 10, 1768, ownership of the works was conveyed to Joseph. Another of John Potts's sons, Isaac, was the owner of the gristmill by 1773, and not long after that time built a stone house (later to be rented by George Washington for a headquarters) on the eastern side of Valley Creek near the point where it empties into the Schuylkill. A somewhat larger house was built nearby as a summer residence for David Potts, who lived for most of the year in Philadelphia.[6] Within a short time, however, William Dewees, a son-in-law of John Potts, had acquired this house and, along with Isaac Potts, joint ownership of the forge.[7]

The coming of war in 1775 gave the establishment at the mouth of Valley Creek an increased significance. As a source both of military materials and of flour for the troops, it became an important part of the American army's supply base. Despite being a Quaker, William Dewees accepted appointment as a colonel of militia, and a large part of the production of the forge and gristmill was devoted to support of the war effort. One account says that a hundred men were working fourteen hours a day on production of munitions.[8]

Valley Forge was thus a logical military objective when the fighting moved into southeastern Pennsylvania. Following the Battle of Brandywine on September 11, 1777, elements of the British forces making a wide swing around Washington's army in a drive toward Philadelphia reached Valley Forge on September 18, and were joined by reinforcements early on September 20. On that date, John Montrésor, captain of Royal Engineers, wrote: "At 2 this morning the guards moved and posted themselves with the Light Infantry at the Valley Forge. Waggons employed in carrying off from the magazine there, the rebel stores." Before leaving early on September 23, the British burned the sawmill and the forge.[9] The gristmill, however, was spared (it survived until 1843, when it too was destroyed by fire).[10]

OPENING OPERATIONS

Following the outbreak of hostilities at Lexington, Massachusetts, April 19, 1775, the Americans enjoyed a considerable run of success. Fort Ticonderoga and Crown Point, two British strongholds near Lake Champlain, were captured. Although an attempt to invade Canada failed, Boston was invested and, on March 17, 1776, the British were forced to evacuate the city and take to sea. In George Washington the Continental Congress had named a commander-in-chief to direct the motley collection of untrained militiamen which comprised the army, and some faltering steps had been taken to establish a foundation for a military force—the Continentals—in the service of the Congress instead of that of the respective colonies. In June, a British amphibious attack on Charleston, South Carolina, was decisively beaten off. And then, on July 4, 1776, Congress declared American independence.

But when the scene of action shifted to the vicinity of New York City, the tide began to turn. American forces were badly defeated at the Battle of Long Island in late August, 1776, and in mid-September were driven off Harlem Heights, just above Manhattan. This was followed by another defeat, at the end of October, at White Plains. Crossing the Hudson, Washington retreated through New Jersey and then, in December, crossed the Delaware into Pennsylvania.

Confident that the Americans were as good as beaten, the British forces now settling into winter quarters scattered through New Jersey from Trenton to New Brunswick grew careless. Washington was quick to take advantage, carrying out his famous Christmas surprise attack across the Delaware to strike the Hessian garrison at Trenton, following this with another victory over a British force at Princeton. At this, the senior British commander (Sir William Howe) withdrew his army to the vicinity of New Brunswick. Washington went into winter quarters at Morristown, New Jersey, and military operations for all practical purposes were suspended by both sides.

As spring approached, the British began probing and raiding, but the main army remained in and around New Brunswick, relatively inactive. Thus, Washington gained time to rebuild his army, which through the winter had been decimated by desertions and the departure of men whose short-term enlistments had expired. By the end of May his force had grown to some ninety-two hundred men.[11] Also during May there had been a steady flow of European volunteers. Some of these—artillerymen and engineers in particular—were welcome, but many proved to be a disruptive influence. Few of them could speak English, and to a man they had been promised high rank by the American agents in Paris who had recruited them. They demanded precedence and seniority over veteran if professionally uneducated American officers, who were understandably resentful.

Aside from the difficulties of rebuilding and providing support for the army, Washington faced complex strategic problems. The British War Office was planning a campaign to fragment the colonies: General John Burgoyne was to march south from Canada, Colonel Barry St. Leger was to drive southwestward along the St. Lawrence River and Lake Ontario through the Mohawk Valley, and Howe was to move north up the Hudson, with all three columns converging on Albany. It was a sound plan, but apparently Howe was given discretion as to whether or not to participate, and chose to pursue an independent course. Washington saw the danger, but as long as Howe remained stationary, the American army had to stay in position to meet whatever move he might make. American forces deployed in the upstate New York area would have to deal with Burgoyne and St. Leger.

The fact that Howe did not move meant that the other options available to him remained open. Because the British virtually controlled the sea, it was quite conceivable that Howe might choose to move against the undefended southern states or, by way of Chesapeake or Delaware bays, against Philadelphia. Washington, lacking sufficient strength to take the initiative himself, could only wait and watch.

Finally, in July, Howe's forces boarded ship and sailed. Concluding that their objective was probably Philadelphia, Washington began shifting his army southward. Then, early in August, he learned that after appearing off the entrance to Chesapeake Bay, the British transports had headed out to sea again. With no way of knowing where Howe might next appear, Washington ordered his army into camp about twenty miles north of Philadelphia and awaited developments.

THE CAMPAIGN OF 1777

It was two weeks before there was any firm information. But this time there was a verified report that the British fleet was inside Chesapeake Bay, heading northward. Evidently, Howe planned to disembark his troops at the northern end of the bay and march overland toward the city, only forty miles distant.

Despite having sent units to reinforce the Americans facing Burgoyne, Washington still had some eleven thousand men, although only about nine thousand of them were armed.[12] Now that he had some idea of the British objective, he marched his men south to meet Howe's invasion, passing through Philadelphia on August 24. By August 28, the British had landed and moved on to camp at the Maryland village called Head of Elk (modern Elkton). The main body of the Americans, with outposts thrown out toward the British camp, lay near Newport, about thirteen miles northeast.

Not until September 8 did Howe make any significant move. During the night of September 9, his army reached Kennett Square, but Washington had kept between the British and Philadelphia. Having crossed Brandywine Creek, the American army was massed around Chadd's Ford, six miles east of the British position. Based on information available to him, Washington believed that he had adequate defenses at all the fords over the creek. Thanks to the help of Tories who knew the area, however, Howe's intelligence was better. On September 11, while a division under the Hessian Baron Wilhelm Knyphausen feinted an attack against Chadd's Ford which completely preoccupied Washington's attention, Howe took the rest of his force upstream, crossing at unprotected fords, and then turned southward to hit the American right flank. Although surprised, the Americans put up a sturdy defense and, with reinforcements brought by Washington, were able to check the momentum of the British assault in hard fighting that lasted till nightfall. In the confusion a few units panicked—one regiment broke when fired into by another American unit, and one of the French volunteers, Brigadier General

Prud'Homme de Borre (who for this later resigned in the face of threatened dismissal) led his men in precipitate flight. On the whole, however, the army performed with considerable credit, and Washington rapidly reassembled his men at Chester.

Howe did not move again until September 16, when he headed northwestward by way of West Chester and on toward the Chester Valley. Washington, however, had made a corresponding move and was in position to block any further advance. Just as the British were beginning to engage the American outposts, both armies were drenched by a sudden, torrential rain. With their powder dampened, they broke contact.

Leaving a division under Brigadier General Anthony Wayne to watch the British, Washington moved north and west to get closer to the army's major depot at Reading so that he could resupply his troops. The extensive marching and countermarching had been hard on clothes and shoes, and many of the men during the hot days of the autumn had lost or improvidently thrown away their blankets. The Schuylkill River was at flood stage, and from his new position Washington was confident that he could readily block the fords which now offered the only means of crossing it. Also, while Howe lay relatively inactive in the Chester Valley, the Americans set about removing stores from locations now within British reach.

One of these was the storage depot at Valley Forge. Among other materials, it held thirty-eight hundred barrels of flour, twenty-five barrels of horseshoes, twenty hogsheads of resin, several thousand tomahawks, and quantities of soap, candles, and entrenching tools.[13] On September 18, Captain Henry Lee with a detachment of Light Horse and Lieutenant Colonel Alexander Hamilton, of Washington's staff, were sent to take these supplies to a safe place. Assisted by Colonel Dewees and Isaac Potts, they were in the act of loading stores onto barges when a British raiding party galloped up. Outnumbered, Lee and his cavalrymen paused only long enough for a brief exchange of shots before escaping to the west, while Hamilton and Dewees took flight across the river.

With Howe now on the move toward Swede's Ford, Washington sent a series of orders to Anthony Wayne to follow the British column and harass the baggage train at its rear. However, several of the couriers were captured, alerting Howe to the fact that Wayne was somewhere behind him. The British commander sent out scouting parties which eventually located Wayne's forces, hidden in a wooded ravine in the hills near Paoli.

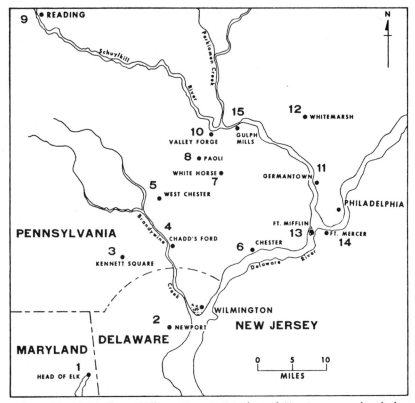

Aug. 28, 1777, Gen. William Howe's British and Hessian army landed at
Head of Elk, Md. (1), to begin an advance on Philadelphia. George Wash-
ington's American army took up a blocking position near Newport, Del. (2).
Sept. 9, Howe side-slipped to Kennett Square (3); Americans deployed at
Chadd's Ford (4), but were defeated there in the Battle of the Brandywine,
Sept. 11. While Howe continued northward via West Chester (5), Americans
reassembled at Chester (6), then marched northwest to intercept Howe near
White Horse (7), but heavy rain prevented a battle. Leaving Anthony Wayne's
division near Paoli (8), Washington crossed the Schuylkill to protect his major
supply depot at Reading (9) against possible attack. Sept. 20, British troops
surprised Wayne at Paoli, moving on to occupy and burn Valley Forge (10).
Feinting toward Reading to cause Washington to leave downstream fords
uncovered, Howe crossed the Schuylkill, moving Sept. 25 to defensive positions at Germantown (11) and sending a detachment to occupy Philadelphia.
Oct. 4, Washington's attack on Germantown was beaten off. Howe moved
into Philadelphia, and Washington occupied a line of hills at Whitemarsh
(12). Howe then struck at Forts Mifflin (13) and Mercer (14), which were
blocking the Delaware. Fort Mifflin was abandoned Nov. 15, Fort Mercer
Nov. 20. On Dec. 5, Howe moved against Whitemarsh, but fell back to
Philadelphia Dec. 9. On Dec. 11, Washington left Whitemarsh, crossing the
Schuylkill near Gulph Mills (15), where the army camped until Dec. 19, when
it went into winter quarters at Valley Forge.

Meanwhile, on September 19 the main American army waded chest-deep through the Schuylkill at Parker's Ford and moved on eastward. In a march lasting till after midnight, the men forded Perkiomen Creek and made camp on its eastern bank. As the army passed through Trappe on its way, Pastor Henry Muhlenberg (whose son, Peter, also a clergyman but now a soldier, commanded one of Washington's brigades) was shocked as he watched the disgruntled soldiers. "Instead of prayers," he wrote disapprovingly, "we hear the dreadful national evil, curses."[14]

Throughout the same day Wayne's force lay hidden, confident that it was secure, waiting vainly for the British to resume their march so that their baggage train would be vulnerable. Then, an hour before midnight, a five thousand-man British force under General Charles Grey stealthily left Howe's camp. Completing the movement unde-tected, this force smashed down from the north, surprising and killing the American outposts and driving in to overrun Wayne's camp, bayo-netting Americans who stood to resist and setting fire to the hastily abandoned huts. This blaze, combined with the flames of the camp-fires, threw enough light to aid the British task appreciably.

Wayne rallied enough of his men to form a rear guard to cover the westward retreat of the rest of his force, and the British did not pur-sue. Of Wayne's fifteen hundred troops, fifty-three had been killed, about one hundred wounded, and seventy-one captured[15] (including two officers, one of whom was a French volunteer), along with a num-ber of loaded supply wagons. British casualties were only one officer and two enlisted men killed and seven wounded.[16]

On September 21, the day after the Paoli "Massacre," Howe marched his army toward the Schuylkill to bivouac along a line from modern-day Phoenixville eastward to just beyond Valley Forge. From this point, he could move against either Reading or Philadelphia. Which-ever Washington chose to defend, the other would be left open. Exploiting Washington's dilemma, Howe sent a detachment westward in a feint which convinced Washington that Reading was the British objective. While the Americans pushed up the Schuylkill to block what they thought would be Howe's line of advance, the British crossed the river unopposed at Fatlands Ford; by 3 p.m. on September 23, they had established a defensive line at Norrington (modern Norristown), between the American army and Philadelphia.

Washington had been outmaneuvered. His men were exhausted and the rigors of the campaign were reducing them to scarecrows—in a letter to Congress of that same day, Washington reported that at least one thousand of the troops had no shoes. There was no way now that Howe could be prevented from entering Philadelphia at his leisure.

Washington had already acted to see that as much food, clothing, munitions, and other supplies as possible were removed from the city. The Liberty Bell was taken to Allentown. Congress had decamped and had reconvened at York on September 18. Few of the inhabitants except Tories and neutrals remained. What had been, after London, the largest British city in the English-speaking world was now reduced to a population of about twenty thousand.

But Howe remained cautious. He waited until September 25 to move to Germantown, halting there with the main body of his army while a detachment under Lord Cornwallis made a formal entry into the city on the morning of September 26.

Howe was right to be cautious, for within days Washington was planning to attack him. Reinforcements had raised the American strength to some ten thousand men, only three thousand of whom were militia, concentrated around Skippack. On October 2, Washington advanced a few miles farther, to Methacton Hill, the jump-off point for his attack.

The British at Germantown were holding a line extending northward from a point near but not on the Schuylkill. Washington's plan was complicated, envisioning a coordinated attack to achieve a double envelopment. Specifically, one column of Continentals, under General John Sullivan, would move eastward to hit the British center; another column of Continentals, under General Nathanael Greene, would circle farther to the north and then strike south to hit the British right flank; a force of Maryland and New Jersey militia would march still farther to the north, then turn southwestward to strike the right rear of the British position; and General John Armstrong's Pennsylvania militia would advance along the Schuylkill to force their way past the British left and move into position to block any retreat toward Philadelphia. The attacks were to start simultaneously at 5 A.M. on October 4.

After dark on October 3, the American troops moved out. Sullivan's column, accompanied by Washington, had no difficulty and was in its assault position on schedule. Unfortunately, however, the civilian guide with Greene's force lost his way, and this column was seriously delayed. Although Washington had received no word from Greene, he assumed that the troops on the north were ready to strike and ordered Sullivan to launch his attack according to plan.

A heavy fog hampered the movement but contributed to the complete surprise which Sullivan's men achieved. Even so, the British out-posts reacted quickly and gave stubborn resistance as they fell back on the main British force two miles beyond, in and around the village of Germantown itself. Some of the outposts took shelter in the Chew mansion, a solidly-built stone house. Instead of bypassing this strong-point, Washington diverted troops to try to storm it; the rest of the line drove on, and before long was threatening to cut through the main British position.

On the north, Greene finally arrived, almost an hour late, but he smashed in vigorously. However, as a court martial later found, General Adam Stephen, who commanded the right wing of Greene's column, was drunk, and under his confused orders his troops angled off to the southwest and moved into the rear of the element of Sullivan's column that was commanded by Wayne. In the fog, thickened by clouds of powdersmoke, Stephen's men mistook Wayne's forces for enemies and opened fire. Wayne's troops, believing themselves under British attack, halted and fired back. Sullivan's men, to Wayne's right, also halted their forward drive. The sound of the firing in the rear of the forward elements, along with the noise of the engagement at the Chew House, gave rise to the belief that the attacking force was being encircled. With their ammunition running low, the Americans began falling back.

The rest of Greene's column on the north continued its attack, and its leading elements pushed all the way to the center of Germantown; but with no more American pressure from the west and the arrival just then of British reinforcements from Philadelphia, there was no chance of holding on, so Greene ordered a withdrawal.

As for the other parts of the plan, the militia column on the north never reached the battlefield; and except for an exchange of cannon fire with the British left-flank units, Armstrong and the Pennsylvania militia did not get into action.

The whole operation was over by 9 A.M., with the Americans in full if not disorderly retreat. The British followed for nine miles, but were slowed by the bad state of the roads and discouraged by cannon fire from the rear guard which Wayne had formed. The retreat continued as far as the western bank of Perkiomen Creek.

Although the attack on Germantown had failed, it had come close to succeeding. This near-victory, capped within a few days by the con-clusive victory over Burgoyne's invading force at Saratoga, had a major impact in European capitals, and France began seriously considering the possibility of direct intervention. Washington described himself as "mortified" by the outcome, but his situation was by no means bad. Some militiamen went home, but even more came in, and Washington was able to deploy a line of Pennsylvania militia patrols above Philadelphia to cut off any traffic from the city to the north. The main American army blocked British access to sources of supply to the west, and British foraging south and east was inhibited by the Schuylkill and Delaware rivers, respectively. The Delaware did offer a potential water avenue of communications from the city, but it was blocked by Fort Mifflin, located on an island near the western bank, and Fort Mercer, on the New Jersey side.

Realizing that Howe would now concentrate his efforts on reducing the Delaware River forts, Washington detached as many troops as he dared to reinforce their garrisons. Indeed, a major British effort against the forts began on October 8. Washington could do no more to provide direct assistance, but he drew his lines even closer around the landward side of Philadelphia and intensified his measures to interdict communications from the city.

On October 15, news arrived of General Horatio Gates's victory over Burgoyne; this was celebrated formally on October 18 with religious services, featuring what Washington specified were to be "short discourses" by the regimental chaplains,[17] followed by an artillery salute of thirteen guns and a *feu de joie* of musketry—a running volley, delivered somewhat raggedly by the untrained troops—and capped with three cheers led by the Major General of the Day. Then, on November 2, Washington moved once again, taking up a strong position on an east-west line of three hills near Whitemarsh.

The forts on the Delaware still held out against mounting attacks by British land and naval forces. By the night of November 15, however, Fort Mifflin had been battered into ruin by incessant artillery bombardment and had to be evacuated. Fort Mercer's garrison, threatened by the approach of a massive British force, held until the last possible minute, slipping away on November 20. What was left of the American naval forces in the Delaware fell back up the river to Bristol, above Philadelphia. With a water route now open to Howe, there was no longer any possibility of starving the British out of the city.

At Whitemarsh, the main body of the American army stood fast. The troops had not been paid since August; rations were short, and there was no salt to season what food the men did have. Whiskey, an important element of the American diet at that time and particularly sought for in view of the cold and exposure, was in very short supply.[18] About one man in four was barefoot,[19] which led Washington to offer a ten-dollar reward for the best design of a substitute for shoes, to be made from rawhide.[20] Morale, which had remained high despite the autumn's hardships and setbacks, began to decline, with a consequent rise in desertions.[21] Nonetheless, when advance word arrived that a British attacking force was approaching, there was a feeling of renewed confidence. "We had a commanding position," one soldier wrote later. "We were sure of giving them a drubbing. . . ."[22]

The attack began early on December 5 with a skirmish between outposts in front of the American right flank, but this was soon broken off. Except for an exchange of cannon fire on the following day, there was no further action until the morning of December 7, when Howe probed tentatively toward the American left front. Once again, after some skirmishing in that area and toward the American center, the British fell back. Howe remained inactive during December 8; on the next day, having decided that the American position was too strong, he started his troops back toward Philadelphia.

But Whitemarsh was too close to Philadelphia to be secure against sudden raids, and on December 11, Washington started the army westward to cross the Schuylkill as a first step toward selecting an encampment for the winter. Reaching Matson's Ford (modern-day Conshohocken), General Sullivan and the leading division were part way across the river when they found a strong British force on ground dominating the road at the Gulph (Gulph Mills), just beyond the ford. Sullivan pulled back his men and moved four miles upstream to Swede's Ford, where the army camped for the night. At sunset the next day, after two improvised bridges had been built and scouts had determined that the British near Matson's Ford were gone, the army started across the river, taking all night to complete the move to occupy the abandoned British camp at Gulph Mills.

The baggage train, "with both tents and kittles and beds," a soldier diarist wrote,[23] had already been sent still farther west to avoid risk of capture. "To the sixteenth," he continued, "we had no tents nor anything to Cook our provisions in and that was Prity Poor for beef was very leen and no salt nor any way to Cook it but to throw it on the Coles and brile it and the warter we had to Drink and to mix our flower with was out of a brook that run along by the Camps and so many a dippin and washin it which maid it very Dirty and muddy."

Even though the wretched state of the men in the wind and freezing rain which came on December 16 compelled Washington to order the tents returned, Gulph Mills was not suitable for winter quarters, and a firm decision on another site still had not been made.

The problem was not easy. The encampment had to be far enough from Philadelphia to preclude successful British surprise attacks. But the farther west the army moved, the more of Pennsylvania would be exposed to British foraging. According to some accounts, Pennsylvania's governing authority (the Supreme Executive Council) threatened that if Washington moved farther than twenty-five miles from Philadelphia it would be compelled to withdraw its vital logistical support and even remove the Pennsylvania troops, amounting to three of Washington's fifteen infantry brigades and about a fourth of his artillery and cavalry strength. Some advisers recommended Wilmington, Delaware; but its terrain was too flat to be easily defended and the army would be seriously vulnerable to attack while marching there. Others proposed a line from the Reading supply base to Lancaster, or from the Schuylkill to Bethlehem; but either choice would be too far away for the Supreme Executive Council, and would leave at least a dozen vitally important iron forges open to the British, and in both cases the troops would be housed in civilian residences. There was a basic aversion to billeting soldiers on civilians, many of whose houses were already overcrowded with refugees. General James Potter, of the Pennsylvania militia, argued this point with little grammar but great eloquence:

> I assart winter Quarters is not to be found In the state of pennsylvania my reasons for this Assartion is, the Capitale is in possession of the Enemy, and there is such large numbers fled from it, and the neghborhood adjasent, and the Towns and viledges along the River Dalawar, that all the Towns and Viledges back in the Country are full of Refugees all redey. What will be dun with those people Turn them out of dores to make Room for the Solders god for Bid it—that would be cruily unexamplified by Gen¹ How himself.[24]

Valley Forge offered some answers. Some eighteen miles from Philadelphia, it was too far for easy British attack yet close enough for the Americans to interfere with foraging parties from the city. General Louis Duportail, the very capable French volunteer who was Washington's Chief of Engineers, had already found that the ground offered naturally strong defensive possibilities. Shelters could be built, so that no civilian houses need be requisitioned. Also, it was hoped that the rich farmlands of the area would provide food for the men and forage for the animals.

Before any move could be made, however, the army had to carry out the orders of Congress to observe December 18 as a day of thanks-

George Washington reviews the troops at Valley Forge, a painting by William T. Trego.

giving and prayer. Despite the men's misery in another day of cold rain, they were formed to listen to the "suitable discourses" of their chaplains. For some, this was followed by a fairly festive meal. One participant reports that he ate "a Roasted pig."[25] Others, dependent solely on the commissary issue, fared far less well—in at least one regiment, the ration was half a gill of rice and a tablespoonful of vinegar.[26]

On the following morning, the sick and wounded left for Reading. At 10 A.M., the rest of the army—about eleven thousand men[27]—left for Valley Forge, five or six miles away.

The road was deeply rutted and the ruts were frozen into rough edges that were hard enough on shoes; for the more than two thousand soldiers who were barefoot, every step must have been agony. To make the troops even more miserable, a cutting wind was blasting a fine, light snow. Nevertheless, the last of the men reached the new campsite by nightfall, less than seven hours after the leading elements had started from Gulph Mills. Under good conditions, eleven thousand men in Indian file (the only formation the men yet knew) would need something on the order of six hours to complete such a move. Even formed in two files, one on each side of the road (as may well have been the case), they could hardly make the march in less than four hours. Considering the weather, the road, and the condition of the men, this performance is impressive indeed.

Independence National Historical Park Collection

Nathanael Greene, by Charles Willson Peale

Independence National Historical Park Collection

Anthony Wayne, by James Sharples

II

Unless Some Great And Capital Change Takes Place . . .

INITIAL ARRANGEMENTS

A LTHOUGH Washington had issued explicit instructions concerning the order of march, it appears that no advance party had been sent ahead to guide the arriving regiments to their respective bivouac sites. Certainly, the arrival of the army came as a complete surprise to the inhabitants of the Valley Forge area.[1] With night falling as the last files moved in, there was considerable confusion. Finally, tents were pitched, but canvas offered little protection against the bitter cold and many of the men, having no blankets, sat up through the night huddling beside fires to keep from freezing.[2] There was almost nothing to eat, and for some men nothing even to drink. A parched Connecticut soldier asked two men with filled canteens where they had found water; unwilling or unable to tell him, they refused to give him a drink and finally sold him a "draught" for three pence in Pennsylvania currency—all the money he had.[3]

Starvation was an imminent possibility. Because rations were not only issued but also were largely procured by brigade commissaries, distribution was often unequal, and in some brigades there were literally no provisions to issue. The situation became so desperate that, on December 21, what looked like an incipient mutiny developed as the chant spread through the camp, "No meat, no meat," accompanied by caws and owl hoots. There was no insubordination, but a clear warning had been served that the army's very survival as an organized body was at stake. Further, when a British foraging party was reported to be heading toward Darby and Washington issued orders for a striking force to be formed to attack it, he was told that there was not enough food to provision even a small force for field operations. In the entire camp there were only twenty-five barrels of flour, and not a single animal that could be butchered. Worse, there were no prospects of new supplies. Reporting to Congress, Washington wrote that "unless some great and capital change takes place . . . this Army must inevitably . . . starve, dissolve, or disperse. . . ."[4]

Exposure was as great a threat as starvation. On December 20, orders were issued that the division commanders "accompanied by the

Ingenieurs are to view the Ground attentively and fix upon the proper spott for hutting so as to render the Camp as strong & inaccessible as possible. The Enginieurs after this are to marke the ground and direct the Field Officers to Superintend the Building for each Brigade where they are to be placed."[5] The snow had ceased on the 19th, but still covered the ground and the weather remained cold. By December 23, strength returns show that lack of shoes or clothing made 2,898 men unfit for duty—almost one man in four.[6] With no time to lose, those who were able began energetically to build shelters. Tom Paine, visiting the camp about this time, wrote to Benjamin Franklin that "They appeared to me like a family of beavers; every one busy; some carrying logs, others mud and the rest fastening them together."[7]

On Christmas Day there was not even any rum to permit the issue of the gill of spirits with which Washington habitually noted special occasions. Washington himself invited the Marquis de Lafayette and the various Officers of the Day to join him for dinner, but was able to serve only small portions of veal, mutton, potatoes, and cabbage, with nothing but water to drink.[8] Furthermore, that day brought a heavy snow which continued through the night to accumulate some four inches.

Washington, having promised the soldiers to "share in the Hardships and partake of every inconvenience,"[9] had been living in a tent with no heat except from a fire outside. Now, however, he found it impossible to handle his multifarious administrative responsibilities without better shelter. As many of the other generals had already done, he sought housing in one of the local civilian residences. In his case, for a hundred pounds in Pennsylvania currency[10] he rented the house belonging to Isaac Potts from its current tenant, the twice-widowed Mrs. Deborah Hewes, whose first husband had been one of Isaac's brothers.[11] Mrs. Hewes moved in with the family of her brother-in-law, William Dewees.[12]

The weather continued very cold and the snow stayed deep on the ground. Three days after Christmas there was another four-inch snow, with temperatures dropping even lower, and still more snow beginning on the afternoon of the 29th. By December 30, the Schuylkill had frozen solid and the snow was half a foot deep. But a start at least had been made on shelter for most of the men. Rations, although irregular in arrival and inadequate in quantity, had continued to come in. At New Year's, it was possible to issue each man a gill of rum. As one of those present wrote in his journal, "We got some Spirits and finish'd the Year with a good Drink & thankfull hearts in our new Hutt. . . ."[13]

SHELTER

By no means all of the troops were in "hutts" by December 31, but substantial beginnings had been made.

Even before leaving Gulph Mills, Washington had issued instructions that the soldiers were to be formed into twelve-man squads, each charged with building its own hut. These shelters were to be made of logs chinked with clay, and were to be six and a half feet high, fourteen feet wide, and sixteen feet long. They were to be aligned along company streets, with doors (made of boards, if available, otherwise of split-oak slabs) facing the street. There would be a fireplace in the rear, made of wood and "secured" with clay. Behind the enlisted men's huts was to be a line of huts for officers. These were to be of the same design and dimensions; but instead of twelve men, each would house the officers of two companies (six to eight men), the three field officers (major through colonel) of a regiment, the members of a brigade staff, or one general officer.[14]

Roofing was a problem, and was left to individual ingenuity. However, Washington offered a hundred-dollar reward for the best suggestion for a substitute for roofs made of boards.[15] One soldier reported that his squad roofed its hut with leaves,[16] but presumably he referred to evergreen branches, as the deciduous trees would certainly have lost their leaves long before December. As another expedient, the quartermasters were ordered to procure "large quantities" of straw for roofing and bedding; if the local farmers objected to providing straw on the excuse that the wheat had not yet been threshed, "the Straw will be taken with the Grain in it and paid for as Straw only."[17] In some cases the huts were roofed with tent canvas—an unauthorized practice which was promptly forbidden.[18] In still others, use was made of saplings or of earth covered with splints.[19]

Timber was plentiful in the hills. Tools and nails, however, were in extremely short supply;[20] draft animals were few in number, and those few were starved and weak, so the men had to harness themselves to the logs they cut and drag them through the frozen mud to the building sites.[21]

As was to be expected from a body of half-trained and highly individualistic men, at least some of the squads followed their own notions despite Washington's precise specifications, and the huts actually constructed seem to have varied considerably from the prescribed pattern.

By no means all rose to the designated six and a half feet. Perhaps to use fewer logs or perhaps to reduce the area exposed to the winds—

increasingly piercing as the hills were denuded of trees—many of the huts were dug in so that their floors were almost two feet below ground level. Whatever its advantages, this practice contributed to the dampness and general unhealthfulness of the huts to the extent that the heat from the fireplace was unable to warm the entire interior.

The lateral dimensions also varied. Hut areas in different parts of the encampment excavated during the course of archeological projects have revealed wide diversity of size and shape, many of them being substantially smaller than the prescribed fourteen by sixteen feet, one being only eight by ten feet. Obviously, several of these structures could hardly have housed twelve men; it is possible, therefore, that these were officers' quarters rather than squad huts. On the other hand, considering the fact that at least two men could sleep on the floor and others would be absent on details such as picket, guard, and fire-keeping, even the smallest of these buildings could probably have accommodated the number of squad members who were off duty at any given time.

Diversity is also reflected in the fact that, of the hut areas studied, one had its fireplace on the side; in several others, the fireplace was on one of the rear corners; and in the huts with fireplaces in the rear, some were flush with the wall and others were recessed into alcoves.

Uniformity, however, was far less important than speed in getting the troops under shelter. Washington offered a twelve-dollar prize for the first well-constructed hut to be completed in each regiment,[22] and by nightfall of December 21—the same day as the protest chant—one structure was finished.[23] By December 29, little over a week later, some nine hundred huts were under construction. Within three weeks, a substantial number of the shelters were finished,[24] but it was February 8 before Washington reported that "most of the men are now in tolerable good Hutts."[25]

"Tolerable" was the key word. There was no ventilation except through the doors—while some huts did boast windows, these were covered with oiled paper,[26] and it was not until May 14 that orders were issued for each hut to have two windows.[27] Because some of the chimneys were poorly constructed, or because the wood burned in them was green, many of the huts were filled with smoke which hampered breathing and inflamed the men's eyes. On the other hand, one man commented that "We have got our Hutts to be very comfortable, and feel ourselves happy in them."[28]

One problem which developed as the winter progressed, however, was filth inside the huts. As early as January 7, an order directed that the Regimental Officers of the Day would make morning and evening inspections of the interior of each hut to check its cleanliness.[29] From archeological excavations, however, it is obvious that in many cases the bones from meat that had been eaten were simply tossed into a corner. Apart from the menace to health which this practice represented (which will be discussed in a later chapter), the combination of decaying animal matter with the crowding together of unwashed men clad in filthy rags must have created an extremely fetid and noisome atmosphere. As spring came on and the comprehensive training program initiated in March began to take effect, it is possible that there was some improvement in the sanitation inside the huts. Obviously, however, the problem still existed as late as May 27, for on that date an order stated that the mud chinking between the logs of the huts was to be removed "and every other method taken to render them as airy as possible." It went on to direct that "They also will have the Powder of a Musquet Cartridge burnt in each hutt daily to purify the Air or a little Tar if it can be procured."[30]

Furnishings were necessarily sparse. The archeological studies indicate the probability that slender poles, anchored in small holes in the floors, were set in place to support bunks or other items of furniture. Straw, to the extent available, provided a mattress of sorts.[31] Each squad was allotted one pail, contingent on the quartermaster procuring a sufficient supply.[32] One account also states that each hut had a rough plank table.[33]

At best, the soldiers were poorly housed. In a letter of January 6 to his wife, Lafayette described the huts as "little shanties that are scarcely gayer than dungeon cells."[34] Bad as they were, however, they did accomplish their purpose, which was to shelter the troops through the winter. The inadequacies of this shelter were certainly a factor in the high rate of disease and death which the army experienced, but the other factors—starvation rations, insufficient clothing, and wretched hygiene compounded by medical deficiencies—would undoubtedly have taken a heavy toll even by themselves.

SUBSISTENCE

The prescribed daily ration for a soldier was a pound of bread, a pound of either meat or stockfish, a pint of milk, a quart of beer, peas, beans, and butter.[35] In practice, of course, the stated ration was meaningless, with the reality being the bare subsistence level that could be maintained primarily by the army's own efforts.

Almost immediately after the army arrived at Valley Forge, detachments had been sent out to the countryside to operate on a protracted basis, collecting foodstuffs and sending them back to camp.[36] But the supply of meat continued to be extremely limited. On the first two days of 1778 there was none at all available for issue.[37] On January 5, Washington wrote that even with "the most sparing oeconomy" the meat supplies would not last more than two days. In the nick of time the situation was briefly eased when, on January 7, some "loyal Philadelphia women" drove in ten teams of oxen that could be slaughtered for food. Further supplies must have continued to come in, for on January 13 Washington issued an order condemning butchers who had "extorted money from the soldiers" for the "plucks" of the beef—i.e., hearts, livers, and lights—and directing that these items be issued in rotation to the various companies. Also, on Monday, January 19, he directed that provisions be issued in sufficient quantity to last through the following Thursday. Less than a week later, on January 24, he was able to prescribe a schedule of issues: three days' rations to be issued on Mondays and four on Thursdays.[38] Erratic deliveries must have still been the rule, though, for on January 28, Washington informed the Congressional Committee on Conference which had come to Valley Forge to investigate conditions that the total available resources in cattle amounted only to ninety head.[39]

February brought no improvement. The Congressional committee reported that on February 11 some brigades had received no issues of beef for four days.[40] On that same day, a meeting of general officers was held to alter the basic ration, in theory, to a pound and a half of flour, a pound of beef or three-quarters of a pound of salt pork, and "a certain amount" of spirits. But on February 15, some units again had gone four days—some even longer—without meat. On February 19, Washington reported again that some men had received no provisions for several days.[41] General Nathanael Greene, writing to General Henry Knox, on leave in Boston, a week later stated that the troops had gone seven days without meat, but that he and some other officers had taken up a collection which had provided a degree of temporary relief.[42]

From this statement it seems clear that at least some foodstuffs were available for purchase from the farmers of the area. The problem, as will be discussed later, was in procurement and issue through official channels. Officers were entitled to draw rations—indeed, as part of their pay they were entitled to draw multiple rations, the number being prescribed on a graduated scale in proportion to rank. However,

as early as January 3, Washington stated that "he doth strongly recommend" that officers draw only the ration required for personal con-
sumption, receiving their remaining entitlement in money rather than
in kind.[43] Unlike the men, therefore, they were not completely dependent on the commissary issue; to the extent that their pay was not
in arrears or that their private funds permitted, they could thus offset
the inadequacies of the issue rations.

With March, the situation finally began to ease. An order of March
15 concerning the disposition of hides implies clearly that slaughtering
of cattle by brigade commissaries was a daily affair.[44] During the last
week of the month a herd of approximately five hundred cattle was
expected.[45]

Conditions became even better in April. Pennsylvania troops, knowing of the annual shad run in the Schuylkill, led the way in a massive
netting of fish which went on for weeks. Meals not only gained welcome variety by the addition of fresh fish, but large stocks were salted
and preserved for the future. In the middle of the month the ration
was fixed at a pound and a half of flour or bread, a pound of beef or
fish or three-quarters of a pound of pork, half a pint of peas or beans,
and one gill of whiskey or spirits—and although the announcement
was qualified by the statement that these quantities would be provided
"agreeable to . . . the state of stores in Camp," for once there seem
to have been reasonable prospects that the issues would actually be
made. On April 19, Washington made the statement, unthinkable in
January or February, that the army now had prospect of more cattle
than it needed, and concerned himself with making sure that only
well-fattened stock was sent to Valley Forge.[46]

Shortages of other foods had been as drastic as those for meat. At
the beginning of the year, officers of Greene's division had no vege-
tables at all.[47] For some units there were a few cabbages, potatoes, and
turnips, but these were grossly inadequate. A small supply of onions
was issued during the second week in January. Eggs and coffee were
unobtainable; a little tea was available, but at greatly inflated prices—
and in gold, not Continental currency.[48]

The gristmill at Valley Forge has been mentioned, and ovens had
early been built in the basement of the Dewees House, which was referred to as the "Bakehouse" as early as January 4.[49] Even so, supplies
of flour were uncertain, and for six consecutive days during the month
of February none was received. Rice, to the extent available, was procured for the sick, but Indian meal was authorized as a substitute
which, it was noted, "can at all times and under all circumstances

be had."[50] When all other supplies failed, the troops were usually able to collect enough flour to make "firecake," a concoction of flour and water, more often than not unsalted, baked on a griddle.

The shortage of salt was a matter of concern. Although the commissaries were directed to issue it at the rate of one quart for every hundred pounds of fresh beef,[51] a shortage was mentioned on January 31, in conjunction with attempts to find a method of manufacturing "this necessary essential article."[52]

Procurement of spirits was another problem which, because of the place of liquor in the eighteenth-century diet, was considerably more serious than it might seem. On January 1, Nathanael Greene relayed to Washington the "murmurs" of his officers; "They think by proper exertions spirits may be procured to alleviate their distress," he wrote, and suggested that stocks be requisitioned from known locations and allocated at the rate of thirty or forty gallons for the officers of each regiment. "This," he concludes, "would give temporary relief, and the present dissatisfaction seems to be so great, it is absolutely necessary to take some measures, if possible, to silence as many of the complaints as may be."[53] Perhaps in response, on January 10 Washington authorized the issuing commissary to sell the officers, on credit, "small proportionable quantities of Spirits." But on January 23 he was reporting that the army at Valley Forge was short of whiskey.[54] On the 31st, each officers' mess in all brigades was issued a gallon of spirits "against these raw and bitter days."[55] On January 26, each brigade had been directed to appoint a sutler and prices had been fixed for various types of liquor; the price of whiskey was set at six shillings per quart. The price list, however, failed to include rum, French brandy, "Jinn," spirits (West Indian rum), and "Cyder Royal," with the result that by March 22 it had been found that "the Vendors of these articles have taken advantage, and therefore Sell them at yᵉ most Exorbitant Rates." This resulted in the establishment of a price scale for these items, effective March 28. April 16 brought another price list, dropping the price of whiskey, apple brandy, and other spirits to four shillings a quart.[56]

Even water was hard to obtain. The limited number of wells within the camp's boundaries was completely inadequate for so many men. Regiments camped near the Schuylkill were fortunate in this respect. Valley Creek, on the other hand, was a poor source because buckets had to be carried up the steep slopes of the ridge which separated the creek from the main camp; Trout Creek was easier of access, but many of the units could use it only at the price of a long walk, with considerable risk of spilling on the way back. Snow could be melted, but it soon became too foul to be drinkable. Ignorant of the hazards to their health, men fell into the habit of making use of the nearest puddle, until the practice was banned by an order of March 19, which stated:

> The Commander in Chief directs, that the officers will be very attentive to yᵉ water which their men Drink. The little springs about the Camp, from which they have been accustom'd to supply themselves during yᵉ Winter, will, in their present State, become extreemly Impure, and pernicious, in yᵉ approaching warm season. As it is a matter so essential, It is expected that yᵉ officers will, without Delay, take measures to provide good Water for their men, by having yᵉ Springs open'd and clean'd, and well sunk in proper places, with Barrels to preserve them, taking care to have them frequently emptied and cleans'd, to prevent any accumulation of Filth.[57]

Just as food shortages created hardships for the troops, shortage of forage brought extreme hardship for the army's horses. And poor as were the huts of the soldiers, the horses had no protection at all against the rigors of elements and the season.

To ease the requirement for fodder at Valley Forge, before Christmas Washington had transferred the Light Horse units under the Polish volunteer, Count Casimir Pulaski, to the Trenton, New Jersey, vicinity.[58] Even so, by January 3 many horses at Valley Forge had already died from starvation and exposure. Three days later, Washington issued orders prohibiting retention of all "private horses"—that is, all except those expressly authorized as mounts or for hauling cannon or supply wagons. On January 9, "to prevent the waste of Forage," another order directed the brigade quartermasters to build feed racks for the horses of their organizations. This directive, as well as the one of January 6, appears to have been ignored, for on January 12 a somewhat more peremptory order stated that "The Brigade Qʳ Masters are to see that the orders of the 9th instant for building racks for the horses be properly complied with and the Waggon Masters pay proper attention to the Horses, and that every Soldier caught on horse back be immediately confined and punished."[59]

Reinforcing the desire to reduce the demands for fodder was the fact that horses gave the men mobility; and some of the starving troops, assisted by the lack of control over their movements which was commonplace at that stage, were ranging out into the surrounding countryside to forage on their own. This practice not only interfered with the official procurement system but often crossed the borderline to become outright looting.

As will be described in a later chapter, discipline was lax in many respects, and on January 26 some feed racks had not been built. On that day, Washington directed with impatient curtness that they "are once more ordered to be set up without further Delay." [60]

As another measure, an order of January 18 directed that on January 19 and 20 all privately owned wagons and horses in the camp were to be turned over to the Quartermaster General for reallocation according to the requirements of the army as a whole. [61]

Notwithstanding these actions, the supply of forage continued to be inadequate through February and into March. As horses died, the army's potential for a spring campaign seriously deteriorated. In a report of February 12, the Committee on Conference warned Congress that if the British were to attack Valley Forge successfully, the American cannon would probably be captured simply because there were not enough horses to move them. [62] Two weeks later, the artillery commander, General Knox, wrote that hundreds of horses had starved to death. [63] The problem loomed large in Washington's correspondence of February 8 and February 15. [64] Aside from the impact of the loss of mobility on the army's effectiveness, the fact that many carcasses of dead horses lay unburied was a serious menace to the troops' health.

April brought considerable improvement in the ability to provide for the horses that had survived the winter, and the end of the month saw the first arrivals of remounts, with more coming in about the middle of May. By May 24, it was possible to return cavalry units to Valley Forge, and the three "divisions" into which they were organized, commanded now by Colonel Stephen Moylan, were reassigned there. [65] Through the winter, however, it is estimated that no less than fifteen hundred horses had died. [66]

CLOTHING

Even at the start of the campaign, only a small number of the army's units had anything approaching uniforms, and these varied greatly in color and design from regiment to regiment. The hard service and long marches of the autumn had worn out shoes and reduced the clothes to rags. At Valley Forge, the damp, rainy weather through much of the winter further rotted fabrics, and the frozen ruts which covered large parts of the campsite caused shoes to wear out even more rapidly.

From the beginning of the encampment, clothing shortages were acute. "Few men have more than one Shirt," Washington wrote on December 23, "many only the Moiety of one, and Some none at all." On December 27 and again on December 29, he listed the most pressing needs as being for shoes, stockings, and blankets.[67]

Pending receipt of new supplies, steps were taken to safeguard what was already available. Noting that men who had adequate clothing when hospitalized were "in a manner naked" by the time they were well, thus requiring a new issue of clothing before they could return to duty, Washington directed that thenceforth all men entering hospital would be accompanied by a list of "every article of Cloathing[,] those Lists signed by the Captain or Officer Commanding Comp^{ys}"; any unit commander failing to provide such lists was threatened with a general court martial.[68]

Another expedient adopted early (it was announced on December 31) was a program whereby the hides of cattle slaughtered for food were bartered for shoes. The official rates, fixed on January 18, were four pence per pound for hides and ten shillings a pair for shoes.[69] In the long run, this was to prove very effective; however, considering the army's previously noted shortage of cattle persisting for several months and the facts that at these rates one pair of shoes cost thirty pounds of rawhide and that more than two thousand men were already barefoot, it is obvious that the barter program could not have provided a rapid solution to the army's problem.

Some supplies of cloth must have been available, or at least anticipated, on January 1, for on that date each regimental commander was directed to report the number of "taylors" in his organization. These men were to be given instruction on approved standard designs for the garments they produced. Perhaps there was no connection, but on January 4 Washington announced that he was "pained" to learn that "Some Tents have already been cut up by the Soldiers and disposed off,"[70] presumably for clothing.

On orders, parties had been sent into the countryside to seize clothing from the population. Admitting that the result had been "the greatest alarm and uneasiness, even among our best and warmest friends, spreading some disaffection, jealousy & fear in the people," Washington regretted the necessity but stated flatly that "The alternative was to dissolve the Army."[71] A ray of light came about this time, however, when on January 1 General William Smallwood, commanding a force stationed at Wilmington, Delaware, reported the capture of the British brig, *Symmetry*. Among her other cargo, she was carrying

"Scarlet, Blue, & Buff Cloth, sufficient to Cloath all the Officers of the Army, & Hats, Shirts, Stockings, Shoes, Boots, Spurs, &c. to furnish compleat Suits for all."[72] Disposition of these items was to cause considerable bickering, but they did help to ease the shortage.

Because the Continental regiments were provided by and identified with individual states, it was to their respective states that they had to look for their principal source of supplies. There was a consequent variation in the degree of shortage from one regiment to another. The Virginia units, better equipped to begin with than some of the others, were in less desperate straits.[73] On December 29, an officer of the 2d Continental Light Dragoons was sent to Boston to procure clothing for his regiment. That same day, Washington sent circular letters to all the state governments, pleading for clothing.[74] On January 6, requests for donation of clothes for the sick were also broadcast through the churches.[75]

There were glimmers of hope. A notice of January 14 announced that "The Cloathier has some Stockings suitable for Officers at reasonable prices,"[76] and by January 24, some clothing supplies had come in for the Connecticut regiments. But these were by no means enough. Noting the continuing need, Washington recommended the manufacture of coats "like a sailor's Sea jacket," which could incorporate "a small cape and cuff of a different colour to distinguish the Corps."[77] Possibly with this in mind, he issued orders the same day excusing the tailors of each regiment from other duties "to be imploy'd in making up the Cloaths for their respective Reg^ts."[78]

The extent and urgency of the army's needs demanded extreme measures. When enlistments of some of the Virginia troops expired, an order of January 21 required them to turn in their blankets before leaving for home. This order must have caused complaint, as a brigade order two days later offered a somewhat conciliatory explanation. "The distress for blankets," it said, "makes it necessary to retain those the Soldiers have who is then discharged. This the Brigadier hopes will be readily complied with By the men who are going home in order to afford more Comfort to their Brother Soldiers who keep the Field." But it concluded firmly that "the Commanding Officers of Reg^ts are therefore directed to Stop all the Blankets."[79]

January 27 brought word that a number of wagonloads of clothing for the Virginia regiments were on the way. They had overturned while crossing the Susquehanna River, but would be brought to Valley Forge as soon as they could be dried out.[80] On the same day, Congress approved payment for 650 suits which Anthony Wayne had ordered from a Lancaster manufacturer to clothe his Pennsylvanians.[81]

Despite these signs of progress, conditions over-all remained appalling. Sentries were seen standing on their hats to shield their feet from the cold of the ground. Not only were the sick robbed of their clothes while too ill to protect them, but the bodies of many of those who died were buried naked, stripped to provide for the survivors.[82] Since numerous deaths were from contagious diseases, this practice contributed to the spread of infection. As of February 5, there were 3,989 men who, lacking clothes or shoes, were unavailable for duty.[83] It is somewhat incongruous that on this same day, Washington was detailing his view of what the clothing policy should be. He believed that issues should be made regularly twice yearly, on July 1 and January 1.

> In June should be given a waistcoat, with sleeves, flannel, if it is to be had, two pair of linen overalls, one shirt, a black stock of hair or leather a small round hat bound, and a pair of shoes. In January, a waistcoat to be worn over the former, close in the skirts, and double breasted resembling a sailor's, to have a collar and cuff of a different colour, in order to distinguish the regiments, a pair of breeches, woolen overalls, yarn stockings, shirt, woolen cap, and a blanket when necessary. Watch coats ought, if possible, to be provided for sentinels.[84]

It was inevitable that the uneven nature of the states' responses would cause difficulty. A supply of clothing delivered to the camp early in February was issued according to the greatest need. Subsequently, it developed that this supply had been provided by the Pennsylvania authorities for Pennsylvania troops, so on February 10 it was recalled to be issued as intended. On February 19, however, Washington wrote that the Pennsylvanians were still grumbling that they had not received all the issue to which they were entitled.[85]

Despite some progress, shortages persisted. Soon after the middle of February, Lafayette wrote to his wife that "The unfortunate soldiers are in want of everything; they have neither coats, hats, shirts or shoes."[86] And on February 24, Captain John Laurens (one of Washington's aides) wrote to his father, Henry Laurens, President of Congress, that he had only one pair of wearable breeches.[87]

For some of the troops, though, things began to look up. On February 23, a meeting of brigade commanders was held to determine how to allocate a recently arrived supply of clothing so as to alleviate the most pressing shortages. Based on this determination, issues were actually made on February 25.[88] While the situation was somewhat better, Washington's efforts the next day to reclaim a supply that had gone astray make it clear that the need was still acute.[89]

About this time a newly arrived foreign volunteer who called him-self Friedrich von Steuben was inspecting the troops with a profes-sional military eye. Considerably later, he wrote of the army at Valley Forge that

> The men were literally naked, some of them in the fullest extent of the word. The officers who had coats had them of every color and make. I saw officers at a grand parade at Valley Forge mounting guard in a sort of dressing gown made of an old blanket or woolen bed cover.[90]

Appalled as he was by the conditions, he was impressed by the men's dedication. He told Washington that no European army would hold together in the face of such hardships.[91]

By March, some supplies were beginning to arrive from France, although on March 6 Washington complained that the French shoes were poor, "affording little more than a day's wear." On the next day he reported that a supply of cloth had come in from Virginia.[92] However, units such as the artillery regiments, drawn in several instances from more than one state, were still constituting a problem[93] and the sup-ply of blankets continued to be less than adequate. As the month wore on, though, the situation improved rapidly. Indeed, the troops were accused of selling their clothes to buy liquor, and Steuben, now acting as the army's Inspector General, felt it necessary to put a stop to the practice by ordering show-down inspections in all units.[94] A brigade order of April 3 makes reference to clothing provided for sale to officers of the Virginia regiments,[95] and on the same day Washington reported that while the Continental units were still not fully supplied, the militia units which were operating in conjunction with his force were being adequately provided for. Shoes for officers and a limited supply of worsted stockings were listed as available at the "Cloathiers Store" on April 5. Three days later, the basic needs had been so well filled that Washington was able to begin trying to stress efforts toward achieving some degree of uniformity.[96]

This is not to say, however, that even the theoretically prescribed clothing allowances were generous. On April 6, Congress had approved for issue to each new recruit in Pulaski's "legion" (i.e., a combined cavalry and infantry unit corresponding roughly to a "regimental combat team" or "combat command" in more modern parlance) one stock, one cap, one pair of breeches, two pairs of stockings, two pairs of gaiters, three pairs of shoes, and one pair of buckles; in addition, to insure well-groomed soldiers, each man was to be issued one comb.[97]

On April 17, supplies of clothing donated directly to Washington by patriotic civilians had become so great that he protested because they were not contributed through the designated supply channels. And less than two weeks later, on April 29, supplies were so ample that many of the soldiers were issued new shoes. More supplies arrived from France, but as late as May 21 some men lacked shirts, and no reserve stock of this item was available.[98] On June 18—on the very eve of the army's final departure from Valley Forge—there were still upwards of a hundred men who were unable to march due to lack of shoes. This was a far cry from the two thousand barefoot soldiers who had stumbled into the camp the previous December 19, but it shows that the problem of clothing shortages at Valley Forge was never completely solved.

Remedies and Expedients

Clearly, the army energetically sought to meet its needs that winter as far as possible through its own efforts. By means of Washington's letters to Congress and to the governing bodies of the states, and through the observations of the Congressional Committee on Conference, the requirements were reported to the responsible authorities. At the same time, no one sat by and waited for the shortages to be supplied.

Almost at the very beginning, on December 22, it was announced that a bridge would be built across the Schuylkill to provide access for supplies from the north, since the Fatlands Ford would be blocked when the river froze. General John Sullivan, notable for his energy, was in charge of construction; but even his vigorous efforts were hampered by bad weather, the shortage of materials and tools, and the competition with the other commanders—trying to finish the huts—for the more skilled carpenters. Even so, before the end of January, he had completed a rough but usable span. Lacking iron spikes, the builders had used pegs to hold the flooring to the stringers. The bottom of the bridge was only six feet above the river's surface, and in 1779, high water carried the whole structure away.[99] Still, it had served its purpose.

In order to make better use of the resources of the surrounding area, on January 20 Washington ordered the general officers and brigade commanders to meet to consider "the expedience of opening a publick Market, in Camp." For some reason this meeting was postponed until January 24. Evidently, satisfactory arrangements were made, for on February 8 an order announced that the following day a market, with prices specified, would be opened at "the Stone Chimney Pickett"; the schedule provided for regular operations at that location on Mondays and Thursdays, across the Schuylkill at a spot near the end of the bridge on Tuesdays and Fridays, and near the Adjutant General's office on Wednesdays and Saturdays.[100] On February 9, a heavy snow made movement difficult and the new program got off to a poor start; but in time it became highly effective. By mid-April, all personnel were prohibited from leaving the camp to buy necessities, as these were considered to be fully available from the markets.[101]

Besides encouraging farmers in the immediate vicinity of the camp to bring in their produce to sell to the troops, and sending permanent parties out into the outlying areas as procurement agents, Washington had detachments ranging even farther afield. In February, for example, General Wayne was sent with some five hundred men into southern New Jersey to round up whatever cattle he could. Unfortunately, this expedition was only partly successful. For one thing, many New Jersey farmers hid their livestock, and Wayne was able to find only 130 head. The British learned that he was in the area and sent a two thousand-man force to trap him, but a daring bluff by Wayne and Pulaski (who had come from the Trenton area to reinforce him) led the British to retreat back across the Delaware. Then Wayne divided the cattle, sending eighty-five ahead and following later with the rest, but the first herd fell into British hands, so that the effort of nearly a month yielded only forty-five head of cattle.[102]

Reference has been made earlier to the program for bartering rawhide for shoes. Another economy was directed in an order of January 12, aimed at saving dirty tallow and ashes to make soft soap, and at "imploying proper persons to boile the Oyle out of the Cattles feet and preserve it for the use of the Army." This effort was temporarily frustrated by the lack of kettles for boiling, but within a week that shortage had been partially solved and on February 1, brigade quartermasters were notified to draw their proportional share of 320 kettles that had been received.[103]

Because the Valley Forge area had long been settled, it was to be expected that larger game had virtually disappeared. Small game animals remained, however, and the troops did exploit this resource. Archeological studies of hut areas have identified the burned bones of squirrels, rabbits, and opossum or racoon. The advantage taken of the shad run was mentioned earlier. On still another occasion there was a flight of wild pigeons, flocking in vast numbers so near the ground that men were able to knock them down with clubs and poles.[104]

Despite their hardships, it appears that there were limits beyond which the soldiers at Valley Forge would not go. Considering the degree of famine and the poor survival prospects of the horses, it might be expected that the troops would have had recourse to eating horsemeat. There is no written record, however, that they did so, and excavation of offal pits has found only two horse skulls, suggesting that for whatever reason, the men did not resort to eating their horses except on a very limited scale.

Underlying Causes of Shortages

Expedients, however, could not affect the fundamental causes of the shortages, and consequently could provide only partial solutions.

The acute deficiencies of food and clothing from which the army suffered so miserably throughout its winter at Valley Forge were not due to any general lack of supplies throughout the United States as a whole. On the contrary, within all the states, including Pennsylvania itself, quantities of cloth were adequate and supplies of food were ample. A soldier assigned to one of the permanent procurement squads in the countryside who from late December until the end of April was stationed at Downingtown, little over a dozen miles from the camp, stated that "We fared much better than I had ever done in the army before, or ever did afterward. We had very good provisions all winter and generally enough of them."[105]

The organization which Congress had decreed for procurement of supplies was ill conceived, over centralized, and inefficient. These inherent defects were made worse by the fact that much of the time the administration of this organization was inept or indifferent, and in some instances corrupt. The root cause of the army's difficulties in the winter of 1777-1778, however, was the basic inability of the transportation system to meet the requirements of the situation. Thus, even the best administrative system would have been able to make the lot of the army little better.

The existing road net was limited, and the quality of such roads as did exist was abysmal. In wet weather they were deep in mud, and in dry they were cut by hard-baked ruts. Such a situation was not inadequate for a relatively sparse population that was to a considerable extent self-sufficient in terms of basic necessities. For manufactured goods and for preserved foods, the principal avenue of transportation had been the sea. But a concentration of eleven thousand men far exceeded the resources of any locality, and the sea was under the virtually complete domination of the Royal Navy.

Foraging by both armies soon exhausted the supplies of the area within reasonable distance of the camp. One diarist observed by December 22 that "The Impoverish'd Country about us, affords but little matter to employ a Thief, or keep a Clever Fellow in good humour."[106] Inevitably, food prices became inflated, and by January 20, Washington was complaining of the "avarice" of the farmers in Pennsylvania and New Jersey who "are endeavoring to take advantage of this army."[107] The fact that the British paid in gold while the Continentals could offer nothing but debased paper currency was also a major factor. Congress had granted authority to Washington to exercise what amounted to martial law, and there are records of numerous Valley Forge courts martial convicting local civilians of attempting to take foodstuffs to Philadelphia to sell to the British commissaries.

The major supply depot at Reading was up the Schuylkill only some forty miles as the river flowed, but during most of the winter the Schuylkill was blocked by ice, or the water was too shallow to permit loaded boats or barges to move. Not till the end of March did moderating weather conditions make river shipments feasible.[108] As for movement over land, not only was it extremely difficult during the winter, but teamsters were hard to find. The maximum which Congress was willing to pay for a wagon, four horses, and a driver was thirty shillings a day, but shortages and inflation drove the prices up and the wagon contractors were not interested in any daily rate of less than forty-five shillings.[109] On February 15, Washington suggested that free Negroes in the southern states be hired as teamsters,[110] but the proposal does not seem to have been acted upon.

In February, a supply of salt pork was located in New Jersey, but lack of transportation prevented it from being brought to Valley Forge.[111] And even to the extent that wagons and wagoners were obtained, the miserable state of the roads caused frequent breakdowns. Loads often were jettisoned by the roadside, and the Committee on Conference reported substantial quantities of abandoned equipment and supplies.[112] On occasion, when breakdowns were threatened by the roughness of the roads, drivers would knock in the tops of the barrels of salted fish or meat in their cargo and drain off the brine to lighten the load.[113] Naturally, the contents spoiled, and more than once, salt fish reaching Valley Forge were so rotten that they were almost liquefied in their barrels.[114]

As was already mentioned, the inadequacies of the commissary and quartermaster procurement systems pale to relative insignificance in the light of the deficiencies in the means of delivering such provisions and materials as were procured. Nevertheless, there were instances of bureaucratic mulishness which seem incredible. One such concerns the attempts of Anthony Wayne to obtain clothing for his Pennsylvania regiments.

Even before the army moved to Valley Forge, Wayne had arranged to buy all the ready-made breeches which could be located in the State, and to get options on cloth for five hundred coats. Quite reasonably, the Pennsylvania authorities overruled him, on grounds that such procurement should be handled through the agencies established for the purpose—otherwise, individual commanders would drive up prices by competitive bidding, with no guarantee of fair distribution to the army as a whole. But when cloth did become available for the Pennsylvania regiments, the Clothier General (a civilian official functioning under Congress) would not release it except to authorized tailors. While Wayne fumed and his troops froze, the Clothier General went on vacation; as he had no deputy, there was no one with authority to make the cloth available even when approved tailors were located. When the Clothier General finally returned to his duties, he still would not release the uniforms because the only buttons available were yellow, while the buttons prescribed for the Pennsylvania regiments were white. Only when Wayne had obtained an official change of the uniform regulations to alter the prescribed color of his division's buttons was he able, at long last, to obtain delivery of this vitally needed clothing.[115]

In fairness, it should be pointed out that there was a general lack of awareness of the extent of the army's plight, and that this was an unavoidable result of a deliberate policy. With British forces in strength only eighteen miles from Valley Forge, it was essential that they not realize the weakness of Washington's army. The Congress and other officials were kept informed by the reports of Washington and the Committee on Conference. Henry Laurens, President of Congress, also received detailed accounts of hardship from his son, John, serving at Valley Forge on Washington's staff. But the price of concealing the facts from the enemy was that the country at large could have little inkling of the actual situation. Unquestionably, this prevented the development of a popular sense of urgency which might have reduced if not fully overcome some of the obstacles which contributed to the army's suffering.

Henry Knox, by Charles Willson Peale

III

The Poor Sick, Suffer Much
... This Cold Weather

THE WEATHER

WHILE there is no complete or precise meteorological record of the winter the army spent at Valley Forge, a reasonably detailed picture for essentially the entire period can be pieced together from diaries, letters, and other records. The only substantial gaps are for the ten days of January 21-30 and the week of February 17-23. Leaving out those days, between December 19, 1777, and the army's final departure from Valley Forge on June 19, 1778, the temperature was above freezing the entire time except for the last thirteen days of December, eleven days each in January and February, and five days in March.

The heavy snow which fell on Christmas Day was followed by another heavy snow on December 28-29, which accumulated to a depth of six inches. This remained on the ground through January 5, but the next day brought warmer weather which, on January 8 and 9, converted the area into a quagmire which must have been at least as unpleasant for the men as frozen, snow-covered ground. There is no record of the weather of January 10, but on January 11 snow began to fall again, continuing through the night. By the time it stopped, it was a foot deep.

Although the next several days saw no precipitation, the snow stayed on the ground until January 17, when the temperature rose again, once more causing deep mud, which lasted through January 20. The weather from that time through the 30th is not recorded, but quite possibly continued with little change, as the last day of the month was marked by a drenching rain that lasted all day.

February brought almost a week of warm and pleasant days. Then, on the 7th, what began as a heavy rain changed to snow as the temperature fell. Again there was a deep accumulation, with the snow continuing through February 9. A thaw began on the next day, with heavy rain causing more deep mud on February 11. Then there was another freeze, with cold, raw days lasting through February 16. No written descriptions of the succeeding week have survived, but the next day for which a record exists—February 24—was marked by sleet and severe cold which continued through the 27th. A brief thaw on February 28 was followed by three days of snow at the beginning of March, and then two days of intense cold.

This gave way to two days of moist, warmer weather, but more low temperatures and snow developed on March 9 and 10. Rain fell all through the next day, and the warming trend which this reflected brought nine days of balmy, spring-like weather with only occasional showers. Leaves began to appear on the trees. March 21, however, was the first of three very cold, wintry days. The weather grew better for the rest of the month, although there was some rain through April 1.

Then once again the weather deteriorated, and from April 2 through April 9 the days were bleak, windy, and raw. For the next ten days there was considerable wind and some rain, but the temperatures were moderate. Once more the days turned cold, with the chill and periodic rains and wind continuing from April 20 through the 25th.

Thenceforth, with the winter well over, the army experienced normal spring weather. There were days of wind and rain, but except for the last five days of May—which were cold and rainy, with the 31st being so chilly that men felt the need for fires—the days progressed from warm to hot.

Summing up, of the eighty-six days for which weather records are available or can be reasonably deduced between December 19, 1777, and March 31, 1778, snow was falling or on the ground during a total of twenty-nine days, and sleet fell on one other. During the same period, there were seven rainy days. There were ten days that the weather was cold, but with no precipitation, and without snow on the ground. By contrast, before the false spring which began on March 12 and lasted through the 20th, there were six days at the beginning of February and two days early in March when there was no rain and the temperatures were almost balmy. On the whole, therefore, the winter of 1777-1778 cannot be considered particularly bad. Unquestionably, weather conditions contributed to the hardships endured by the troops, but this was due not to any unusual severity of the winter. Rather, it was the result of exposure, given impact by the poor shelter, inadequate clothing, and malnutrition from which the men suffered.

MEDICINE AND HEALTH

It has been estimated that some three thousand men of Washington's army died of disease during the winter of 1777-1778.[1] However, statistics are fragmentary. It is even difficult to approximate deaths as a percentage of men falling ill. Here again, statistics are minimal; and to a considerable extent, those which do exist are blurred by the practice which prevailed of consolidating in a single total the figures for the sick and for those who were not available for duty due to lack of clothing. No central burial ground has been found at the campsite, and only some thirty graves have been located. While deaths certainly occurred at Valley Forge, many and perhaps most of the men who died did so at various outlying hospitals in Pennsylvania to which the sick from Valley Forge were sent.

This is not to minimize the situation which existed. At best, ignorance of the causes and proper treatment of disease made for poor conditions of health in the eighteenth century, and in this respect the army reflected the population at large, with the added hazards of injury and combat. For example, a report of August 5, 1777—at a time when no fighting was taking place—shows that over twenty-six per cent of Washington's troops were hospitalized.[2] The hard marching and constant exposure of the autumn's campaign which followed, not to mention the several engagements which characterized it, certainly imposed an additional toll.

Medical science was primitive, and military medicine, necessarily functioning without such amenities and supplies as were available in settled communities, was considerably worse in all armies. Professional standards of performance, and of qualification as well, were far from clear-cut. And the American army, struggling in large part merely to survive, was in no position to insist on even those standards that did exist. This is not to say that the army was without many conscientious and, in the light of existing knowledge, able medical officers; but there were also more than a few who had little formal training, and there were even some outright charlatans.

When army organization became fixed in 1778, each regiment was authorized a surgeon and a surgeon's mate. They were commissioned officers, but held no title of military rank; that they were highly rated is shown by the fact that the surgeon's pay was raised to the same level as that of a lieutenant colonel and that the surgeon's mate was now paid the same as a captain.[3] For the medical department at large there was a Director General, who during the period of the

Valley Forge encampment was Dr. William Shippen. Component elements of the department included the unit medical officers and facilities organic to the army under a surgeon general, and a regional system which operated the larger, more permanent hospitals. The regional organization for the area including Valley Forge was the Middle Medical Department. This was headed, until he resigned in January, 1778, by Dr. Benjamin Rush.

As noted earlier, before leaving Gulph Mills on December 19, 1777, Washington had sent his sick and wounded to be hospitalized at Reading. In theory, therefore, the men arriving at Valley Forge should all have been healthy. In fact, even if no one was sick on reaching the camp, within less than a week a number of men had fallen ill. A regimental surgeon, writing on Christmas Day, stated that "The poor Sick, suffer much in Tents this cold Weather." He went on to comment on the crude treatment that was all that was possible, adding, "But very few of the sick Men Die."[4] On December 26 and again on January 2, Washington was issuing orders insisting on proper reporting of men listed as sick.[5] Clearly, illness was an important problem from the outset.

The situation rapidly grew worse. The February 12 report of the Committee on Conference noted that "sickness and mortality have spread . . . in an astonishing degree," pointing out that "The sick and dead list has increased one third in the last week's return, which was one third greater than the week preceding. . . ."[6]

Throughout the winter, the number of men available for duty continued to be eroded by illness. As late as May 25, Washington was reporting that his freedom to move if the British evacuated Philadelphia was severely limited by the number of sick at Valley Forge itself. Three days later he repeated this observation, and on May 29 he stated that "Near 4,000 men in this Camp are sick of the small pox and other disorders."[7] Although the arrival of substantial numbers of recruits had considerably increased the army's strength, this figure must have represented upwards of a third of the total, and it did not include the large numbers of men in the outlying hospitals. However, those described as "sick of the small pox" appear to be largely men who were suffering the after-effects of inoculation. By May 30, Washington had decided that his only course if he was to pursue the British would be to leave the sick behind, and he directed the brigade commanders to detail officers to remain with them. On June 12, adopting a new plan to eliminate encumbrances to a quick movement, Washington began transferring into the permanent hospitals those ailing troops who previously would have been kept in camp but were too sick to accompany the army on a sudden march. Even so, on June 17, almost on the eve of the final departure from Valley Forge, Washington reported that there were some twenty-three hundred troops sick in camp, representing over eighteen per cent of his total strength of approximately 12,500—and these figures did not include twelve hundred more sick in outlying hospitals within a radius of eight or ten miles.[8]

From the very beginning, the medical procedure had been to move men suffering from more serious ailments out of the camp and into what were called "general hospitals." Reference has already been made to such a hospital at Reading. Others were established at Ephrata, Bethlehem, Easton, Lititz, and Yellow Springs (modern Chester Springs).

Nevertheless, these rapidly became overcrowded. A soldier who had fallen ill before the army left Gulph Mills wrote in his diary that "I with the others of the sick belonging to the Reg't was sent to the hospital at Reddin but when we come thare the sick belonging to the other Right [regiment] had taken it up so we was sent to Dunkertown to the hospital thare."[9] As disease spread, the conditions grew worse: at Bethlehem, for example, between 800 and 900 patients were crammed into space intended for 360.[10] Buildings large enough to accommodate numbers of sick, such as barns and churches, were also converted into hospitals. This was not always accomplished without protest, and some Quaker meetinghouses had to be requisitioned over the objections of the members.[11]

Medicines, food, blankets, even straw for bedding were all seriously lacking. Washington wrote on December 31 that "I sincerely feel for the unhappy Condition of our Poor Fellows in the Hospitals, and wish my powers to relieve them were equal to my inclination. It is but too melancholy a truth, that our Hospital Stores are exceeding scanty and deficient in every instance. . . ."[12] Shortages, combined with ignorance, led to reissue to newly arrived patients of blankets or straw used by men who had died of contagious diseases; this contributed to the tendency for men hospitalized with less serious illnesses to become infected in hospital with often fatal disease.[13]

Death rates were appallingly high. Of five hundred patients entering the hospital at Bethlehem, at least one-third died. One regiment alone, the 9th Virginia, sent forty men to this hospital, but at the time a report of their status was rendered, thirty-seven were dead, one was dying, one was given only a moderate chance for survival, and only one had survived to return to duty.[14] The diarist hospitalized at Dunkertown wrote on February 8 that "I gits better but a Number Dyed. There was between fifty and sixty Dyed in about a month."[15] The North Carolina regiments suffered especially heavy losses, with 204 deaths out of a total of 1,072 men.[16] At Lititz the record was better: of 173 men admitted in the period January 12-22, ten died; of 264 admitted between February 1 and April 20, eighty-three either died or deserted; by the time the hospital was closed on August 28, 1778, little more than eight months after it opened, only sixty-six soldiers had died.[17]

For initial treatment of the sick, or for treatment of those not ill enough to be sent to one of the "general hospitals," an order of January 9 directed the construction of one hospital in each brigade. These were called "flying hospitals," and in accordance with an order of January 13, were to be fifteen feet wide, twenty-five feet long, and at least nine feet high. They were to be roofed only with boards or shingles; sod or dirt was forbidden. There were to be windows on each side, and a chimney at one end. Instead of one such hut as directed four days earlier, each brigade was to erect two, and they were to be located near the center of the brigade area and not more than a hundred yards away.[18]

These also soon became overcrowded, and some of the sick began to be sent to improvised hospitals outside the camp's limits. An order issued by Washington on January 21 pointed out that it was "impossible . . . to make effectual provision for the Sick out of Camp Unless they are sent to the places . . . appointed and furnished for the purpose," and admonished that "A Contrary practice have been attended with great Inconveniency and probably Occasions the Death of many men, many has been sent to the Hosp[l] already Crowded with Patients or to places where no provisions have been made for the Sick." Thenceforth, only the surgeons at flying hospitals would decide what disposition was to be made of each patient. Furthermore, hope was held out that "as soon as possible" medicine chests would be provided the regimental surgeons, making it feasible for more men to be treated without having to be sent away from Valley Forge.[19]

Special efforts were made to ease the lot of the sick in camp. On January 15, the surgeons were directed to assure that the sick were "plentyfully suplied" with straw when they were admitted to one of the flying hospitals.[20] This order, however, was probably little more than a pious hope, because straw continued to be in very short supply. In mid-February, the Committee on Conference attributed many of the deaths that had occurred to the lack of straw or other material to keep the men from having to sleep on the cold, wet ground.[21] Reference was made earlier to the procurement of rice, or Indian meal as a substitute, as food for the sick.[22] Around mid-April, with better supplies beginning to become available, brigade quartermasters were instructed to go into the countryside and contract for regular delivery of milk "and other Necessaries for the Sick." Within less than two weeks, however, the prices had risen sharply; on April 29, an order directed that instead of brigade quartermasters negotiating contracts for these supplies, "a Discreet Serjiant & few men" would be sent out daily to make direct purchases. Late in January, each brigade was directed to detail a captain to visit the brigade's sick in or near the camp to see that they were being cared for as well as circumstances allowed. This order seems to have been less than fully effective, however, for on February 27, one brigade commander was asserting that he had been "much surprised to find so little attention paid" to it, and promising that those guilty of continued dereliction "may depend upon being called to a Severe Account." Nor were the general hospitals forgotten. An order of January 15 sent two senior officers to visit them,[23] although their role was to insure that discipline was being maintained, clothing and equipment accounted for, and desertion kept as low as possible.

The illnesses which affected the soldiers are what would be expected. The men had too few clothes to provide a change while one set was being washed, and the weather was too unpleasant to go without. The spread of vermin[24] and scabies was inevitable. As early as January 8, "being . . . informed many men are rendered unfit for duty by the Itch," Washington ordered the regimental surgeons "to look attentively into this matter and as soon as the men who are affected with this disorder are properly disposed in Hutts to have them anointed for it." Orders were issued for soap to be provided without delay, and for soft soap to be substituted if hard was unavailable. As was previously mentioned, ashes and dirty tallow were to be salvaged to make soft soap as needed.[25]

Exposure and overcrowding naturally made colds epidemic, and these sometimes developed into pneumonia. Unhygienic conditions contributed directly to dysentery, typhoid, and typhus, the two latter being classed together in that era as "putrid fever."

Washington made repeated efforts to improve camp sanitation. On January 7, he directed that a fatigue party be formed "to cause all dead horses in and about the Camp and all Offals to be buried," and that this be a weekly project. Digging garbage pits in frozen ground was no easy proposition, however; furthermore, during the cold weather there was considerable carelessness about using or caring for latrines—"vaults" in the parlance of the times. On February 26, all men were enjoined to use them, "otherwise the Camp will be unsufferable from the Stench . . . and very prejudicial to the health. . . ." Ten days later the warning had to be repeated. On March 13, Washington noted that despite his earlier order, "the Carcases of Dead Horses lay in, or near the Camp, and that yᵉ Offal near many of yᵉ Commissaries Stalls, still lay unburied, that much Filth and nastiness, is spread amongst yᵉ Hutts, which will soon be reduc'd to a state of putrefaction and cause a Sickly Camp." He went on to say that "Out of tender regard for yᵉ lives & health of his brave Soldiery, and with surprise that so little attention is paid to his orders, He again in yᵉ most positive terms, orders & Commands" that the dead horses be buried, and that old vaults be filled and new ones dug. He concluded that "As the above orders are essentially necessary to preserve health in Camp, no plea of Ignorance will be admitted and yᵉ least breach thereof, will be severely notic'd." The implementing order issued in one brigade went a step farther, stating that a guard of three "Sentinals" would be established "to Fire on any man who shall be found easing himself elsewhere than in yᵉ Valts."[26]

Whatever results this achieved were temporary, for on April 10 Washington was again expressing the importance of improved cleanliness of the huts and streets. On the 14th, after a personal inspection, he praised the cleanliness of some areas, but added, "He wishes it had been general; but the case was otherwise; and (notwithstanding repeated orders . . .) the smell of some places intollerable . . . oweing to the want of necessaries, or the neglect of them. He therefore, and for the last time (without proceeding to extremities) requests, that all kinds of dirt, & filth . . . be rak'd together, & burnt, or buried." Further, sentries were to be posted to arrest "any Soldier who shall attempt to ease himself any where but at a proper Necessary, and 5 lashes are to be order'd him immediately. . . ." Perhaps this had some effect. In any case, on May 4, an order stated that "For the sake of Decency, the General hopes, the Commanding officers of Regiments will order their Necessaries to be tied with Boughs, or hurdles. . . ."[27]

Regardless of the measures taken, it is obvious that the problem never was solved. By June 10 the army was forced to move out of the camp into a new area about a mile away, due to the "unwholesome exhalations from the ground." There, "we shall not swallow the effluvia arising from a deposit of . . . filth accumulated during six months."[28]

So far as personal cleanliness was concerned, however, the improvement in the supply of clothing and the onset of warm weather permitted substantial progress. By an order of May 14, troops were excused from other duties on Friday afternoons to launder their clothes, and sergeants were to march the men by squads to bathe in the river; in order to avoid the risk of chills, however, they were warned "to be careful that no man remains longer than ten minutes in the water."[29]

Smallpox was an ever-present and major threat. Although there was a known preventive for it in the form of infecting a healthy individual from a sick person who had a light case of the disease, new recruits had seldom been inoculated before enlisting. Further, there was seldom time to immunize all the troops during the course of a campaign. Thus, there was always the possibility of an outbreak.

Cases of smallpox did in fact occur at Valley Forge, and initially it was to take care of these that the hospital at Yellow Springs was built. The winter encampment, however, was seen as an opportunity to complete inoculations for the army at large. On January 6, regimental surgeons were instructed to report the men of their regiments who had never had smallpox,[30] and a program for their inoculation was begun at once.[31] But supplies were inadequate to care for all the men who would be made sick by inoculation; consequently, the program had to be phased over a period of time—as noted, it had not been fully completed by the time the army was ready to leave Valley Forge for good—and some of the men had to wait, thus prolonging their chances of contracting a severe case through normal contagion.[32] Also, some men were absent on protracted forage details or in outlying hospitals. These, as well as recruits when they began to arrive, all had to be inoculated.[33] The soldier who had been hospitalized at Dunkertown reported on February 28 that "We jined our Reg't and Company and I was anockulated for the Small poxe and had it Prity favorable to what others had it."[34] Despite the crudity and risks of the method, the program must be considered a success, since only ten men of the approximately four thousand who were inoculated at Valley Forge died of the disease.[53]

Another ailment which was to be expected was frostbite, and Lafayette wrote that "feet and legs froze till they became black, and it was often necessary to amputate them."[36] Considering the risk of shock following amputation, especially without anesthesia, and of infection due to lack of antisepsis, it would not be surprising if the mortality rate in such cases was high, but no statistics have survived. What is surprising, though, is that despite the inadequate diet, there is no record that scurvy was a medical problem at Valley Forge, although it broke out among Hessian troops in Philadelphia by January.[37]

The organization for handling the sick was sound enough, even though it proved inadequate to cope with the size of the problem which developed. There was a certain amount of unseemly bickering between regimental surgeons, basically over equitable sharing of work and furloughs, heightened by regional jealousies.[38] There was also a major quarrel between surgeons of the general hospitals and those of the flying hospitals. The general hospital surgeons claimed that patients reached them already all but dead from inadequate care at the flying hospitals; the flying hospital surgeons retorted that supplies and medicines went almost exclusively to the general hospitals, leaving the flying hospitals nothing to work with.[39] In addition to this dispute on a reasonably professional level, there were quarrels on political and personal levels as well. Dr. Rush, who was a member of Congress as well as Physician General of the Middle Medical Department, was one of the faction which sought to replace Washington as commander of the army. Dr. Shippen, his superior in the medical department, was a supporter of Washington. With this motivation, Rush was quick to take advantage of what looked like irregularities in Shippen's procurement of medical supplies for the army, and charged him with fraud. Although eventually a court martial acquitted Shippen for lack of sufficient evidence, this did not occur until 1780, and in the meantime this controversy gave the army surgeons another source of disagreement as they took sides in the dispute.

In most respects, however, the medical officers as a whole appear to have been capable and conscientious. The same is not true, in general, of the soldiers who were assigned as hospital orderlies. The work was unpleasant and the risk of infection was high, so there was a tendency for the more undesirable and irresponsible men to be detailed to hospital duty. As the number of physicians was too limited for them to supervise the orderlies in detail, the sick often received care which was indifferent or—as in the case of re-use of the straw and blankets of men just dead of typhus—fatally harmful. In sharp contrast is the devoted service volunteered by members of the religious communities at Ephrata and Lititz, many of whom became infected, quite a number fatally, with the diseases of their patients.

Significant use of women nurses in military hospitals still lay decades in the future, although there were four women nurses working in the hospital complex at Bethlehem,[40] and on May 31, Washington did urge the employment of as many "women of the army" as could be prevailed upon to accept assignments as nurses. It is probable that he was prompted in this by the desire to free as many soldiers as possible for field service in the forthcoming campaign, for in the same communication he went on to specify that "Orderlies are to be appointed of those who want of Cloathing, lameness, &c, and are unfit to march with the Army."[41]

Reviewing the experience of the Valley Forge winter, the commanders and surgeons cannot be criticized. Within the constraints of the situation, they did the best they knew, in the light of medical science of the time. In particular, they fully appreciated the importance of sanitation, if not the reasons for that importance. The problem was not to develop and announce sound rules. Rather, it was to assure their observation. Compulsion alone could never be fully effective; there had to be individual cooperation. This, in turn, required inculcation of the habit of obedience—a quality which, until the winter at Valley Forge, the American soldiers had not acquired.

Friedrich von Steuben, by Charles Willson Peale

Louis Duportail, by Charles Willson Peale

IV

It Was A Continual Drill

PROVISIONS FOR DEFENSE

AN important factor in the choice of Valley Forge as the site for the winter encampment had been the potential it offered for defense. In establishing the basic camp layout on December 20, each brigade's hut areas had been assigned in terms of its assigned sector of the defenses. While the main effort initially went into constructing huts and completing the bridge across the Schuylkill, by January 15 Washington was urging that "The works mark'd out by the Ingenieurs for the defence of the Camp are to be executed with all possible dispatch."[1]

A tactical analysis of the ground at Valley Forge identifies the critical terrain as the ridge running north from Mount Joy and then swerving northeastward almost to the Schuylkill. Because of the deep and narrow gorge west of this ridge, where Valley Creek flows between Mount Joy and Mount Misery, the position was unassailable from that direction. The left flank—the north side of the camp—was given a degree of security by the river, although the fact that the water was shallow and the stream was spanned by the new bridge meant that there was a potential vulnerability in that quarter. However, the best avenues of approach for an attacking force were provided through the open country to the southeast of the area and along the three roads which penetrated it: one close to the river, leading eastward toward Swede's Ford (approximating the course of the modern Port Kennedy road) ; a second, farther to the south, leading eastward to Gulph Mills; and a third (Baptist Road), running south from the eastern slopes of Mount Joy ridge.

It is obvious from the defensive plan which was adopted that these factors were taken into consideration.

The main line of resistance was established along the forward slope of Mount Joy somewhat above the lower ground through which the Baptist Road passes, and following the contour of the ridge to the bluffs above the Schuylkill. The line itself consisted of a continuous ditch, some six feet wide but only three or four feet deep. It was not designed to provide shelter, but to serve as a dry moat to hamper an attacker; shelter was provided by the mound of earth behind the ditch, held in place by stakes. This line was strengthened at its southern end by dug-in artillery emplacements and a redoubt whose earthen walls rose some ten to twelve feet, called Fort Washington; these covered the entrance of the Baptist Road into the camp area. At the northern end of the line, where it was crossed by the Port Kennedy road, was another artillery emplacement, together with a second earthen fort, called Fort Huntington. About four hundred yards to the front of the ditches, extending northeastward from the eastern foot of Mount Joy for about three-quarters of a mile, was a line of abatis, sharpened stakes set into the ground and angling forward, to serve the same function as a barbed-wire entanglement. Backing this up toward its northern end was another gun emplacement. This whole complex of works was known as the inner line of defense.

The outpost line of resistance, or "outer line," was formed by a nearly straight line of entrenchments stretching from the Baptist Road northeastward almost to the Port Kennedy road, along the lower ridge which formed the hypotenuse of the right triangle which enclosed the encampment. At its northern end were two more earthen forts, Fort John Moore and Fort Mordecai Moore (now called Fort Greene and Fort Muhlenberg, respectively), one on each side of the Port Kennedy road.

On the north, the principal protection was provided by the most ambitious of the earthworks, a star-shaped fort sited on the bluff above the bridge. The northern approach to the bridge was also guarded by a detachment posted across the Schuylkill.[2]

In addition to these fixed positions, pickets were deployed well beyond the camp on the routes leading toward Philadelphia on both sides of the river.

The defensive works were never fully completed, but the project was pursued as persistently as weather conditions and the pressure of other requirements permitted. On January 20, Washington stated that he wanted the officers "to Exert themselves to put the Camp in a[s] defenceless [*sic*] a Condition as possible as soon as may be," and all men not on duty who belonged to brigades in the outer-line sector were directed to fall out every morning at 9 A.M. to work on the entrenchments under the "Superintence" of General John Paterson. Response must have been unsatisfactory, for a week later, a brigade order "earnestly requested" regimental commanders to have their men report daily for this detail. As late as March 27, the main line of resistance was still not finished, and Washington urged the brigade commanders to organize the task and get it completed.[3]

Apparently this appeal gave rise to an excess of zeal, for less than a week later, on April 2, an order stated that "As the Stumps and Brush in front of the new line [presumably, the outer line] afford an excellent obstacle to the approach of an enemy, 'tis expressly forbid, that any of it should be burnt by Fatigue Parties, or others for the distance of extreme Musket-range in front of the line. . . ." On the following day, Anthony Wayne complained that the defenses on this line were "carelessly executed in many parts . . . principally oweing to the weakness of the Stakes, and those of the exterior face being plac'd too Parpendicularly."[4]

Work proceeded apace, and by April 26 the fortifications appear to have been about as fully completed as they were to be. By that time the trenches and abatis along the main line of resistance and the emplacements and redoubts at its flanks were finished and manned.

Fifteen infantry brigades were deployed for the defense. From south to north along the line of entrenchments beginning on the eastern face of Mount Joy were three brigades—William Maxwell's, the brigade formerly under Thomas Conway, and Lachlan McIntosh's brigade, all of Lord Stirling's division. The entire flank along the river was entrusted to the brigades of Jedediah Huntington and James Varnum. From west to east along the outer defensive line were William Woodford's and Charles Scott's brigades of Lafayette's division, Wayne's division of two Pennsylvania brigades, Enoch Poor's and John Glover's unattached brigades, the two brigades—Ebenezer Learned's and John Paterson's—of Johan De Kalb's division, and George Weedon's and Peter Muhlenberg's brigades, comprising Nathanael Greene's division. In addition, there was Henry Knox's artillery brigade, partly located in fixed positions but most of it held centrally to be moved to whatever quarter might require its support.[5]

As March merged into April, Washington considered a British attack to be a distinct possibility, a fact which probably explains the renewed emphasis he placed on completing the works. Sir William Howe stated explicitly to his superiors in London that the position was too strong to assault during bad weather.[6] The coming of spring brought the departure of Howe for England, and Sir Henry Clinton, who replaced him, was intent on getting back to New York with its outlet to the sea. While the Valley Forge defensive works were never put to the test, they served a useful purpose. From Bunker Hill on, even raw American troops had fought well from behind cover, and whatever the weather, it seems highly improbable, once the natural advantages of the Valley Forge position had been strengthened, that any attack within British capabilities at the time could have dislodged Washington's army.

ORGANIZATION, TRAINING, AND WEAPONS

As the spring progressed, there was another reason—perhaps even more significant—why the British could not have driven the Americans out of Valley Forge. This was because, for the first time since the war began, the troops under Washington had begun to be developed into a trained, disciplined, reliable fighting force.

That is not to say that there had been no attempts at training. On the contrary, even during the autumn's campaign, occasions were frequently sought to instruct and exercise the troops in fundamentals. For example, on October 12, Washington observed that "The officers have now an opportunity of attending to the discipline of the Troops," and went on to direct that "Every day, when the weather will permit, the Corps are to be turn'd out and practic'd in the most essential exercises: Particularly, primeing and loading, advancing, forming, Retreating, breaking, and Rallying. No pains are to be Spar'd to improve the Troops in this point." Again, on October 18, he ordered that "The officers Commanding Brigades and Corps, are to draw out their men (excepting those on duty) every day when the Weather permits, to practice the most necessary Manoeuvres. . . ."[7]

However, because units varied enormously in size, it was difficult to achieve any standard of training. Even in theory, the number of men in a regiment or battalion (the terms were used interchangeably) differed from state to state, and in some cases between regiments from the same state. For example, a Connecticut company was supposed to consist of seventy-seven officers and men, with thirteen companies comprising a regiment, totaling (with field and staff) one thousand personnel. A Massachusetts company, by contrast, was authorized sixty-one officers and men, but some regiments had nine companies and others ten.[8] Compounding the problem, few units had ever been at anything approximating full manning levels, and the recent campaign had taken a further toll through casualties, sickness, and desertions. In a number of regiments, short-term enlistments (most of them only for nine months) caused rapid turn over. Many men were absent from their organizations, sometimes for months on end, on detached service as foragers or teamsters, or excused from duty to serve as officers' "waiters" (i.e., orderlies).[9]

At Valley Forge proper, there were seventy-four infantry regiments, plus the artillery brigade, the "corps of artificers" (engineers), Washington's Life Guard, and various headquarters personnel. The total manpower strength as of December 23, however, was only 11,982.[10] On the average, each of the regiments was short almost 400 men of its full complement, although the average shortfall per regiment ranged from 200 men for the units of some states to 560 for each of the nine regiments of the North Carolina brigade.[11] Washington observed on December 27 that regiments were little more than companies in size.[12]

As the winter wore on, some improvements were realized. Washington pressed the states to fill their quotas and urged Congress to approve a standard organization. Men on detached service were recalled, and the number of servants authorized to officers was drastically reduced. In late March, recruits began to arrive, their number increasing through April and May. Somewhat offsetting these gains, however, were the losses from illness and the expiration of enlistments. Also, developing troubles with Tories and Indians on the western frontier had made it necessary in early March to send several units, among them the 8th Pennsylvania Continentals, from Valley Forge to Fort Pitt. On June 17, just before leaving Valley Forge, the army's total strength (including sick held in camp) was only about 12,500.[13]

As early as January 29, Washington asked for authority to standardize brigades at four battalions (regiments) each, and divisions at three brigades.[14] But it was not until May 27, 1778, that Congress approved a standard battalion structure. Each infantry battalion would consist of 582 officers and men, formed in nine companies of 62 officers and men each. Artillery battalions, at 729 personnel in twelve companies, were larger. Cavalry battalions were to have 422 officers and men in six companies.[15] Putting this new organization into effect would take time, but eventually would bring substantial benefits.

Weapons also were a problem. Given the short range and inaccuracy of the musket, the only way to achieve effective firepower was through concentrated volleys. If the bullets were all to strike in the same vicinity, the weapons of any given company had to be of the same caliber and type. But within the army there were thirteen different kinds of muskets and, since they were individually crafted, a great variety of rifles.[16] A single company was often equipped with muskets, rifles, carbines, and fowling pieces. There was a shortage even of these weapons, as no effective attempt was made to reclaim the weapons of men who left for home on being discharged. Finally, such weapons as were available were, too often, improperly cared for, many of them rusty and some incapable of being fired at all.[17]

Infantry tactics of the period placed great reliance on the bayonet. Reloading took so long, and combat took place at such close quarters, that there was seldom time for more than two or three volleys at most. In both attack and defense, therefore, the bayonet was extremely important. Only about half of the American troops had been issued bayonets, and those who did have them had never been trained to use them; their practice, as General Steuben observed disgustedly, was to employ the bayonet as a skewer on which to broil meat.[18]

Here again, persistent effort by Washington brought some improvement, although in the face of substantial difficulties.

On December 21, Washington had observed that "The proper arming of the Officers would add considerable to the army and the Officers themselves derive great confidence from being armed in time of Action." He considered that carrying a musket distracted an officer from his duties toward his men, but being without any weapon had "a very awkward and unofficer like appearance." Accordingly, he directed every officer to provide himself with "a half pike or Spear as soon as possible."[19] On January 18, he instructed the Quartermaster General to order half-pikes ("espontons" or "spontoons") for the officers. These were to have foot-long blades and six-and-a-half-foot staffs. In addition, brigades which had armorers in their ranks were to manufacture bayonets; other brigades were to commission bayonet manufacture by civilian smiths. Over two months later, however, in an order of March 26, he had to remind brigade commanders of these instructions.[20] Neither weapon was popular, and the units had been dilatory about providing them.

Substantial numbers of firearms arrived, although on an irregular basis. On December 21, Washington announced that a French ship, carrying ammunition, cannon, and forty-one hundred muskets, had arrived at Portsmouth, New Hampshire,[21] but that was a long and risky distance from Valley Forge. The *Symmetry,* captured by General Smallwood's troops at the end of the year, yielded over one thousand stands of arms, plus ammunition. Another French ship bringing arms was reported on April 8.[22] This apparently was the cargo including eleven hundred cavalry carbines, but on their arrival at Valley Forge three weeks later Washington wrote that these had turned out to be light muskets, not suited to cavalry at all. In the whole camp at that time there were only 107 carbines; while swords were being manufactured in Virginia, Washington believed that pistols to arm the cavalry would have to be imported. He wrote President Laurens on May 18, urging that arms arriving from France be sent immediately to Valley Forge, explaining that many of the troops (even apart from the recruits who were coming in) were unarmed. On the same day, he had to refuse General Smallwood's request for arms, pleading the scarcity in the main army. A week later he pointed out to General Gates that there were at least twenty-five hundred soldiers at Valley Forge who either were without muskets or who were awaiting the return of their muskets from the repair shops. Not until June 6 could he report to the Board of War that, thanks to the recent receipt of nineteen hundred stands of arms, almost if not quite all the troops had been equipped.[23]

As mentioned earlier, men completing their enlistments had tended to take their weapons with them. "Of all the new [weapons] imported last year," Washington had written on February 8, "it is amazing how few remain. . . ." Even those arms which were turned in posed a problem, as many were damaged and unusable. This was before the days of interchangeable parts, and replacement components for any musket had to be hand-wrought and fitted individually. The troops had hardly arrived at their winter encampment when Washington began a program to repair all the army's firearms. On December 30, he issued orders for all weapons to be inspected and those found in poor condition to be turned in to the armorers.[24] Probably to help in this program, on January 9 he directed all units to report the names of any gunsmiths in their ranks.[25] A directive of January 8 to Henry Knox, Chief of the Ordnance Department (as well as commander of the artillery brigade), required all spare arms to be inspected and repaired—presumably those stored in the magazines at Carlisle, Pennsylvania, and Springfield, Massachusetts, for there were certainly no spares at Valley Forge. On the last day of February, Washington informed the Committee on Conference that unless the Armory Department was improved, spring would find an army enlarged by prospective militia levies and new recruits embarrassingly short of weapons. Large numbers of muskets, he reported to the Board of War on March 6, could not be used as they were in process of repair.[26]

Another recurrent shortage was in ammunition. In a letter of December 28, Washington told General John Armstrong, of the Pennsylvania militia, that a shortage of powder had been temporarily relieved, but the reserve stock was far from satisfactory. He took prompt action to insure that any excess cartridges in the troops' hands

were turned in, but that each soldier's cartridge box was to be completely filled. Damaged cartridges were to be dried and repacked.
This turned out to be a continuing program, and on March 26 he
made a virtue of necessity by directing that sixty-eight of the men not
available for duty because of lack of clothing should be put to work in
the camp "laboratory," preparing ammunition.[27]

Despite these actions, the ammunition problem continued to be a
worry. Repeatedly, orders had to be issued concerning men wasting
ammunition, either through improper care (a difficulty compounded
by the shortage of properly made cartridge boxes) or through unauthorized firing of weapons—usually resorted to as an easy way of clear-
ing a charge from the musket. As late as May 14, Washington wrote
to the Commissary of Military Stores that the reserve stock of only
140,000 cartridges at Valley Forge was entirely insufficient, and on
June 1 he reported to the Governor of New Jersey, explaining a need
for more lead for musket balls.[28] By that time, however, what made the
question of ammunition significant was not any threat to the security
of the troops at Valley Forge. That requirement had long since been
met. What was on Washington's mind was an offensive campaign,
and his efforts had been bent—to considerable effect—toward making
such an operation feasible.

There were other difficulties which also had been overcome.

One of the major defects of the American army up to the time it
reached Valley Forge had been that, to the extent that the troops had
been taught any formations and maneuvers, they had been trained
along widely divergent lines. Each state had its own preferences with
regard to military doctrine. The units of some states had been trained
on the British pattern, others on the French, and still others on the
Prussian. This diversity was serious, since infantry tactics of that
period (and for a century to come) were based on close-order drill.
Without a standard system, cohesive teamwork on the battlefield was
almost impossible to attain. It has been noted that the soldiers knew
how to march only in Indian file,[29] which stretched out each unit for
such a distance that excessive road space was required to move it,
completion of a movement required an inordinate length of time, and
straggling could not be prevented. Granted, the men had been taught
to march in step, thus achieving a steadier, faster rate than by
shambling along at an individual gait, but only to the beat of the
drum, advertising their approach for as far as sound would carry.
Even then, the length of the step and the cadence varied from one
regiment to the next. Files could be deployed into line to right or left,

but line to the front or rear could only be formed with difficulty, confusion, and delay—a serious drawback in battle.

What was certainly one of the worst deficiencies of all was the limited concept which many of the officers had of their duties. Influenced chiefly by the British Army's system, they saw their responsibilities as being restricted to leading their men in combat. All other matters— supervision of training, seeing to the men's well-being, maintenance of equipment, and insuring that directives were in fact carried out— were considered to be solely within the purview of the sergeants.[30] That method would work well enough in an army which, like the British, had a corps of experienced and capable non-commissioned officers, but such a corps was not to be found in the American Army of 1777. The consequences of this default permeated every aspect of the army's activities. Earlier chapters have cited numerous examples, applying to a wide range of functions, of the tendency of intermediate commanders to ignore Washington's directives—not through insubordination, but simply in ignorance that the field and company officers were concerned. In sum, as Steuben observed with only a degree of overstatement, "With regard to their military discipline, I can safely say that no such thing existed."[31]

In one respect, the situation at Valley Forge was not as bad as it seemed. The army was willing and able to learn. What was needed was a man with the professional competence to devise and carry out an effective training program and the judgment and adaptability which would lead Washington to grant him the authority to administer it to all elements of the command. Such a man appeared in the form of Friedrich von Steuben.

The information which was put out when he arrived at Valley Forge on February 23, 1778, was somewhat vague, permitting the inference to be drawn that he was a baron and a lieutenant general in Frederick the Great's Prussian army, which was then conceded to be the finest in the world. Actually, even his name was somewhat spurious. He had been christened Friedrich Wilhelm Ludolf Gerhard Augustin Steube.[32] His father, a Prussian engineer officer, had arbitrarily adopted the particle *von* on the strength of some distaff connections with the nobility. Friedrich himself changed the spelling of Steube to Steuben, thereby adopting the name of a noble Prussian family which had died out a century or so before, and substituted Augustus Henry Ferdinand for Ludolf Gerhard Augustin.[33]

Friedrich had in fact held a Prussian commission from 1747 to 1763, but he rose no higher than captain. He had fought in the Seven

Years War, first as an infantryman, then as a staff officer in the plans and operation section ("quartermaster general's office" in European parlance), and eventually at Frederick the Great's headquarters. His staff title had been Deputy to the Quartermaster General;[34] fortuitously for the future, in the French terminology the Prussian Army used this came out as *lieutenant général quartier maître*.[35]

In 1763 a quarrel with one of Frederick's favorites led to Steuben being dropped from the army. He then obtained a post as Chamberlain at the court of Hohenzollern-Hechingen. In this position he acquired some claim to the title of baron. But in 1777, poverty forced the Prince of Hohenzollern-Hechingen to disband his court. Steuben, having tried unsuccessfully for appointment at the court of Baden and in the armies of France, Spain, and possibly Britain, finally came to the attention of the American agents in Paris, Benjamin Franklin and Silas Deane.[36]

Franklin believed that Steuben had talents the American army needed, but feared that an ex-captain would get little attention. Apparently, he devised the cover story on Steuben's background. It is also probable that he briefed Steuben carefully on the blunders made by self-seeking European volunteers who had previously gone to America. It is a matter of record that he gave Steuben a letter introducing him as a lieutenant general of the Prussian army and equipped him with an aide and a military secretary.[37]

Steuben finally reported to Congress at York on February 5, 1778. He explained that he asked no rank or pay, only expenses and compensation for the German revenues (600 guineas a year) he claimed to have given up; for the rest, he would abide by whatever Congress considered his services to be worth, after he had demonstrated what he could do. Congress was vastly impressed by this contrast with the avaricious attitude of many of the earlier European volunteers, and warmly recommended Steuben to Washington. But Washington had been disillusioned before; while he was cordial to Steuben, he reserved judgment. He recognized clearly that the army needed sound training, and perhaps to test Steuben, Washington asked the Prussian to visit several of the regiments at Valley Forge and report frankly on their shortcomings and remedial steps that Steuben considered necessary.[38]

The idea of appointing an over-all supervisor of training, known then as Inspector General, was not new. Indeed, such a position had been created, and was occupied by Thomas Conway, an Irish-born French officer. But Washington believed that Conway was intriguing for his replacement, and Conway's supercilious attitude antagonized the senior American officers. As a result, even Conway's worthwhile proposals had been ignored or rejected, and on December 31, 1777, frustrated, he had left Valley Forge.[39]

Steuben attacked his task with Prussian thoroughness. His ignorance of English proved no drawback; his military secretary, Pierre Duponceau, spoke good English, and Alexander Hamilton and John Laurens of Washington's staff, both of whom spoke French, helped out. On the basis of his findings, and with advice from Hamilton and Nathanael Greene, Steuben drew up a training plan which Washington approved, naming Steuben as acting Inspector General.[40]

As a start, Steuben asked each brigade commander to select an officer as brigade inspector. Then he began writing a book on drill regulations. Duponceau translated it, and Hamilton and Laurens revised it into American terminology. When each lesson was written, the brigade inspectors made their own copies, which in turn were copied by the regimental and company clerks. As it was already March, there was no time to lose, so Steuben spent the days instructing in one phase of the drill and the evenings drawing up the next phase in the drill regulations.[41]

To demonstrate what he had in mind, he used Washington's Life Guard, a sort of honor company, as a model.[42] As it consisted of only forty-six men,[43] he arranged on March 17 for a hundred men to be added.[44] He took personal charge of instructing these men, scandalizing the British-oriented American officers by taking a musket in his own hands to demonstrate the manual of arms while the soldiers and the brigade inspectors observed.[45] His explosive rage at errors and his flights of profanity in a mixture of French, German, and broken English—it is said that the first English word he learned was "goddam"[46]—delighted the troops and he soon became popular as a "character."[47]

The key to his drill was simplicity. He reduced the number of motions in the manual of arms to ten,[48] and the number of motions to reload from nineteen to fifteen. He imposed a standard pace of twenty-four inches and a cadence of 75 steps per minute—somewhat slower than the thirty-inch pace, 120 steps per minute of modern times, but suited to the rough terrain and the heavy weight of the men's arms and ammunition. He also taught the men to keep step, without relying on the tap of a drum, by watching the officer at the head of the column. He introduced platoon columns, more compact in size and more easily maneuverable, and taught the troops how to wheel in line to the right or left and how to move quickly

Friedrich von Steuben drills recruits at Valley Forge, a painting in the
Pennsylvania State Capitol by Edwin Austin Abbey.

from column into line to front or rear.[49] These were major improvements in battlefield effectiveness.

At Steuben's request, Washington issued an order on March 20 forbidding brigade and regimental commanders to drill their men until the new regulations were issued.[50] This caused some resentment, but was necessary if uniformity was to be achieved. On March 24, the brigade inspectors began training the army as a whole while Steuben kept one step ahead in the training of his demonstration company. By March 28, Steuben's group had progressed to charging by platoons, firing and advancing, and then rushing the objective with the bayonet. He put particular emphasis on bayonet training, including it in every day's instruction. Previously, American troops had never been able to stand up to a bayonet charge, but the confidence which Steuben's training gave them changed this.[51]

Steuben also fought a successful battle to reduce drastically the number of men excused from drill on the various types of detached service, although he did not begin to achieve significant results until May.[52] Already, on April 6, he had used his model company to put on an exhibition drill of what it had learned, impressing the officers and inspiring ambition in the other troops.[53] On April 10, Washington's orders stated that "As marching men by files has an unmilitary appearance, and a tendency to make them march in an unsoldier-like manner, all Parties commanded by Commission'd officers, are to be march'd by Divisions [i.e., in formation], and every Officer commanding a guard, or Detachment, will be very attentive to see, that his men march properly. . . ."[54] The program of training continued intensively, one soldier writing of the period of late April and early May that "I was kept constantly, when off other duty, engaged in learning the Baron de Steuben's new Prussian exercise. It was a continual drill."[55]

Individual drill was only a small part of Steuben's reforms. Uniform formation drill clearly required uniform organization, so Steuben was able to regroup units, at least provisionally, into standardized size.[56] Effective tactical performance demanded standardized weapons, which led to a reallocation to provide reasonable uniformity within any given company. Steuben's example of personal attention to details had a strong influence on the officers, who began to understand and carry out a vastly wider scope of responsibility than they had recognized before. As a result, care of weapons and equipment, individual cleanliness, troop well-being, and personnel accounting were all greatly improved.[57]

Steuben's position was regularized after Conway resigned in late April. On May 6, Washington was able to tell Steuben that Congress had appointed him Inspector General in the rank of major general.[58] It was a widely applauded move at the time, and certainly it was richly earned.

Valley Forge is often regarded as a monument to endurance and dedication, and this is fully justified. But Valley Forge is equally a symbol of the translation of a group of devoted but minimally trained, loosely organized, poorly equipped, and highly individualistic men into a hard-hitting, dependable, efficient army in the fullest sense of the word. It would be wrong to attribute the credit for this transformation exclusively or even primarily to Steuben. As has been shown, many of the reforms were already under way when he arrived, and many were outside his particular sphere of responsibility. Nevertheless, among the factors which brought about the achievement which was realized at Valley Forge, Steuben's contributions loom large indeed.

CRIME AND PUNISHMENT

The fact that the army attained an unprecedented level of training and discipline at Valley Forge did not mean that the commanders were not confronted with a succession of disciplinary problems. On the contrary, even from the incomplete records which have survived, it is obvious that throughout the period of the encampment, numerous offenses were committed. Some of these were purely military in nature, such as desertion and dereliction of duty, but there were also instances of assault, theft, fraud, embezzlement, and various forms of peculation.

One of the most troublesome offenses was pillaging or plundering. The problem, recurrent throughout the fall campaign, continued at Valley Forge. Within a week of the army's arrival, Washington was moved to a flight of outraged rhetoric in a General Order of December 26, declaring that

> It is with in expressable Grief and Indignation that the General has received Information of the Cruel outrages and Robberies lately committed by Soldiers. . . . Was we in the Enemy's Country such practices would be unwarrantable, but committed against our friends are in the highest degree Base Cruel and Injurious to the Cause in which we are engaged[;] they demand therefore and shall receive the severest punishment[.] Such crimes have brought reproach upon the Army and every Officer and Soldier Suffers by the practices of such

villains, and it is the Interest of every honest Man to detect them and prevent a repedition [*sic*] of such Crimes.[59]

After this exhortation, he went on to outline a series of restrictions adding up to a sharp curtailment of freedom of movement by soldiers outside the boundaries of the camp proper.

The measures seem to have had some effect, but on January 20, there was another General Order, threatening punishment for burning farmers' fences, which for understandable reasons the men preferred to the green wood available from the hills. Further problems had arisen by March 3, when orders were issued to establish a guard post on the south end of the Schuylkill bridge to check the passes of troops trying to cross, for "notwithstanding the repeated orders which have been Issued to prevent Soldiers from Straggling . . . the Country round about ye Camp, & to a considerable distance, is full of them"; accordingly, commanders were to tighten restrictions "as well as to prevent ye mischiefs resulting from this pernicious practice to ye Inhabitants, as to be prepar'd at all times against any sudden attempt of ye Enemy." But as late as April 26, Washington learned that men were going through the countryside, "requisitioning" provisions in the Commander-in-Chief's name. Further, restricting the men to the camp area did not completely eliminate the difficulties. On January 6, Colonel Dewees had complained that troops had been making off with whatever of value remained of his forge after the British had burned it. During the next few months he made some progress in reconstruction, but on April 29, he reported again that soldiers had been stealing lumber and stone from his buildings.[60]

Other offenses which provoked General Orders threatening punishment were the violations of rules of sanitation, mentioned in the chapter dealing with medicine and health, and the unauthorized discharge of firearms.

Examining offenses which were considered individually, records in Washington's General Orders and the orderly book of Weedon's brigade show that of 161 military personnel (including civilian employees of the army) tried by brigade, divisional, or general courts martial at Valley Forge, 39 were tried for civil crimes and 122 for purely military offenses.

There were thirteen allegations of fraud, extortion, or embezzlement, eleven of assault, seven of theft, two of perjury or forgery, two of issuing challenges to duels, and one each of attempted sodomy, plundering, and manslaughter. Although drunkenness was a factor in numerous cases, there was only one in which the charge was drunkenness by itself; it

is noteworthy, however, that in this instance the alleged offense was
repeated drunkenness.[61] All told, there were six acquittals and thirty-
three convictions, but in five of the latter, the sentences were reduced
or remitted by Washington. Twenty of those convicted were officers,
ten were enlisted men, and three were civilian employees. A major
reason for the preponderance of officer criminals is that, being in positions of authority, they had opportunities for embezzlement and fraud
which were not available to men in the ranks. Another is that when
enlisted men committed offenses such as petty theft or assault, the cases
tended to be handled by regimental courts martial rather than by
brigade or higher tribunals, and records of the lower courts have not
been preserved.

In the category of military offenses, by far the most frequent charge
was desertion or attempted desertion, of which forty-two cases were
tried. There were eighteen cases of disobedience, insubordination, or
disrespect, sixteen of dereliction or neglect of duty, fourteen of "conduct unbecoming the character of a gentleman," ten of abuse of authority, seven of absence without leave, five of gaming or gambling,
five of cowardice in action (three of which dated from the battles of
Brandywine and Germantown), and five of violation of sundry General Orders. Convictions resulted in eight-six of the cases, with sixteen
of the sentences being reduced or remitted. There were thirty-six
acquittals.

Here again, there are some noticeable differences between the patterns for officers, who accounted for seventy-five cases, and enlisted
men, who were involved in forty-three, the remaining four individuals
tried being civilian employees. Except for one case involving a civilian
employed as a wagoner, all the cases of desertion pertained to enlisted
men. Disobedience or insubordination by enlisted men must have been
handled by regimental courts martial, however, as only two cases of
this offense by enlisted men, both particularly outrageous, were tried
by general courts martial. (It is difficult to believe that in such an
army, there would not have been many more instances of this crime,
even though it is true that several of the previously noted cases of
assault by enlisted men also involved insubordination.) Aside from
one case of dereliction of duty and two of violation of General Orders
by civilian employees, all the remaining cases classed as military
offenses pertained to officers.

This was due to several factors. A substantial number of offenses
applied only to officers (e.g., conduct unbecoming the character
of a gentleman), and others, as noted, were possible through oppor-

tunities available only to officers. Also, officers were often tried for quite trivial offenses which, in a private soldier, would have brought on nothing more than a sergeant's tongue-lashing—for example, Lieutenant Isaac Webb, 7th Virginia, was tried (and convicted) of going on duty in a hunting shirt instead of a coat.[62] Further, he was tried by a general court martial, perhaps because, after January 25, 1778, no officer could be tried without his consent by a brigade or divisional court.[63] A final consideration is that some rules seem to have been enforced only against officers, on the justification that officers were supposed to set good examples.

Gaming offers a prime case in point. It was a practice which enraged Washington, and he had forbidden it by a General Order of January 8.[64] His rationale appears to have been based less on moral than pragmatic grounds: gambling gave rise to quarrels, which would impair morale and discipline. His repeated warnings and threats on the subject suggest that the order was never fully obeyed. The only individuals charged with this offense, however, were officers. When a court martial found an officer guilty of this charge, Washington recognized no extenuating or mitigating circumstances, regardless of the court's recommendations, and any sentence less than dismissal brought on blistering censure of the court in Washington's published review of the trial.

In addition to these cases, there were two trials of women camp followers, accused of conspiring with soldiers to mutiny and desert. One of the women was convicted, the other acquitted.

Further, under the provisions of special regional authority granted to Washington by Congress, twenty-nine civilians were tried for various acts of aiding the enemy by providing foodstuffs, money, or other support. Eight were acquitted and twenty-one convicted, but in five cases the sentences were reduced.

Finally, under this same authority, one civilian was acquitted of giving intelligence to the enemy but convicted of acting as a guide to British troops; and a second civilian (a former ensign, cashiered during the fall for theft) was convicted of spying.

Short of mutiny, no genuine cases of which seem to have occurred, the greatest disciplinary threat to the army's survival during the Valley Forge winter was desertion. The number of cases of this crime that came to trial can give only the barest indication of its frequency. Unfortunately, reliable data on the number of deserters do not exist. Indeed, such data were not always available even at the time. Washington complained on January 21 that, despite repeated orders for brigade commanders to report desertions promptly, "it is by indirect and casual information, that this knowledge comes to the General." [65]

Obviously, desertion was virtually a daily occurrence. On February 2, according to a contemporary news report, no less than ten sergeants, a corporal, and a matross (cannoneer) from the 4th Continental Artillery deserted to Philadelphia; an amended report a few days later changed the number to thirteen sergeants and a corporal, plus a number of privates from other regiments.[66] On February 7, Washington wrote that "The spirit of Desertion among the Soldiery, never before rose to such a threatening height, as at the present time." During the same week, on February 12, Brigadier General James Varnum wrote to Nathanael Greene that desertions were "astonishingly great." On the other hand, Washington was able to tell Greene on February 18 that "There has been no *considerable* desertion from this camp, *to my knowledge within a few days past. . . .*" (emphasis added). And at the end of March he observed that "I am astonished, considering the sufferings the men have undergone, that more of them have not left us." Even so, when writing of the price that had been paid for the lack of clothing, he said that "I am certain Hundreds have deserted" from this cause alone.[67]

The one reasonably precise figure is a Tory statement (hence, perhaps suspect) that between September 27, 1777, and March 26, 1778—only three months of which overlap part of the Valley Forge encampment—1,134 men deserted the American army and came in to Philadelphia, the largest bulk of them being men who had originally deserted from British regiments or had lived in America only a comparatively short time.[68] While it is true that British deserters and former prisoners of war enlisted in American units had an exceptionally high rate of desertion (a fact which led Washington to repeated attempts to halt their acceptance), it does not follow that many native Americans did not also desert. These men, however, tended to return to their homes rather than to go over to the enemy.

The articles of war under which the army operated had been drawn up by a committee of Congress consisting of John Adams and Thomas Jefferson, and adopted on September 20, 1776.[69] Sentences could take the form of reprimands, fines, or death, without regard to rank. Officers convicted of certain offenses could be cashiered or dismissed (apparently there was a subtle distinction), and when an officer was cashiered for cowardice or fraud, his sentence was to include the requirement that his crime, name, place of abode, and punishment be published in the newspapers in and about camp and in his state of residence, after which it would be deemed scandalous in any officer to associate with him (Section XIV, Article 22) —that is, an officer associating with the cashiered officer could be charged with conduct unbecoming the character of a gentleman, conviction of which itself carried a mandatory sentence of discharge (Section XIV, Article 21). Enlisted men, depending on the crime, could be confined, reduced in rank, discharged, or awarded corporal punishment up to a maximum of 100 lashes. Civilians associated with the army were also made subject to the articles of war.

There were fourteen separate offenses for which the death penalty was authorized (dealing with such offenses as desertion, cowardice, mutiny, assisting the enemy, sleeping while on guard, and causing false alarms in camp), but it was mandatory for only two: misbehavior before the enemy or inciting such misbehavior by others (Section XIII, Article 12), and forcing a safeguard (Section XIII, Article 17).

It was also mandatory to cashier any officer found guilty of using "traiterous [sic] or disrespectful words" against Congress or the legislature of the state in which he was stationed (Section II, Article 1), making false certificate concerning absence of any subordinate or false muster of "man or horse" (Section IV, Article 4), knowingly making a false return of personnel strengths (Section V, Article 1), accepting a false enlistment (Section VI, Article 3), refusing to deliver to the civilian authorities any subordinate charged with a civil crime (Section X, Article 1), protecting an enlisted man from his creditors (Section X, Article 2), embezzling soldiers' pay (Section XII, Article 2), being drunk on duty (Section XIII, Article 5), and breaking arrest (Section XIV, Article 20). Discharge was mandatory for a commissary accepting gratuities in connection with mustering a unit (Section IV, Article 6), and dismissal and restitution of costs for an officer embezzling government property or allowing it to be damaged (Section XII, Article 2). Reduction to the ranks was required when a non-commissioned officer was convicted of wasting ammunition (Section XII, Article 2) or of conniving at another soldier hiring someone to perform his duty tour (Section XIII, Article 9). Prescribed fines were mandatory for enlisted men, and reprimands for officers, behaving irreverently in any place of divine worship (Section I, Article 2), and fines for any personnel using any "prophane oath or execration" (Section I, Article 3).

The articles provided for regimental and general courts martial, the latter appointed by commanders of brigades, divisions, or armies, and

consisting of not fewer than thirteen officers (Section IV, Article 1).
In normal usage, however, the term "general court martial" was reserved for courts appointed by the army commander. Regimental
courts comprised at least three but normally five officers, appointed
"for the inquiring into [of] such disputes, or criminal matters, as may
come before them, and for the inflicting [of] corporal punishments
for small offenses. . . ." They could reduce non-commissioned officers
to private, and sentence privates to be discharged; they could try
officers, but could not cashier or dismiss an officer from the service—
such a sentence required a general court martial (Section XIV, Articles 10, 11, and 13).

For the more serious offenses, the system was sound enough. It had
fairly significant defects, however. One was that it authorized no
means of punishing except as a result of a court martial. Washington
took note of this in a report he made on January 29, 1778, stating to
the Committee on Conference that "There are many little crimes
and disorders incident to soldiery, which require immediate punishment and which from the multiplicity of them, if referred to Court
Martials [*sic*], would create endless trouble, and often escape proper
notice. . . ." Later in the same report, he cited another weakness of
the articles of war, pointing out the need for

> . . . a proper gradation of punishments: the interval between a
> hundred lashes and death is too great and requires to be
> filled by some intermediate stages. Capital crimes in the
> Army are frequent, particularly in the instance of desertion:
> actually to inflict a capital punishment upon every deserter
> or other heinous offender, would incur the imputation of
> cruelty, and by the familiarity of the example, destroy its
> efficacy; on the other hand to give only a hundred lashes to
> such criminals is a burlesque on their crimes rather than a
> serious correction. . . . The Courts are often in a manner
> compelled by the enormity of the facts, to pass sentences of
> death, which I am as often obliged to remit, on account of
> the number in the same circumstances, and let the offenders
> pass wholly unpunished.

The remedy, he believed, was that "whipping should be extended to
any number [of lashes] at discretion, or by no means limited lower
than five hundred lashes."[70]

Although the record shows a substantial number of instances when
Washington did reduce or remit sentences, it is also true that he had
been following a deliberate policy of strictness, for in a letter of
November 27, 1777, to the Board of War, he asserted: "That I am

endeavoring to reform the Army, will appear by the great number of severe sentences of Courts Martial that have lately passed."[71]

It is not clear whether he obtained authority for commanders to oppose summary or non-judicial punishment at this time. Manifestly, however, the limit on the number of lashes which could be given was eventually raised, for at Valley Forge he was later to approve sentences of as many as 250 "stripes."

While the army was at Valley Forge, five soldiers and two civilians were awarded death sentences.

A brigade court martial of January 4 convicted John Reily, 2d Virginia, of deserting while on guard and taking two prisoners with him;[72] his execution, set for January 9, was respited to January 10,[73] when it apparently was carried out. Another brigade court martial, held on January 7, sentenced Francis Morris, 1st Pennsylvania, to death for repeated desertions,[74] and presumably he was duly hanged. On February 24, a general court martial acquitted Joseph Worrell, a civilian, of giving intelligence to the enemy; however, his acquittal could have been of little consolation, for the same court sentenced him to death for "acting as guide and pilot to the enemy," and the execution was scheduled for March 3. The only further record of this case shows that on March 2, the execution was "postponed to a future day."[75] As a pardon or remission would have been officially noted, it seems probable that Worrell was eventually put to death.

A month later, on April 6, a general court martial sentenced William McMarth, a matross in Colonel John Lamb's 2d Continental Artillery, to be hanged for desertion. McMarth was a good soldier gone bad: on January 26, he had been convicted of deserting and stealing "an horse" from General Lachlan McIntosh; he had been sentenced to receive a hundred lashes and have "half his pay stoped monthly from him 'till General McIntosh is fully satisfied," but on account of his previously exemplary record, the court had recommended (and Washington had approved) remission of the lashes. For whatever reason, on April 16, after his second conviction, McMarth was granted a reprieve.[76]

Soon after, on April 24, a brigade court martial at Gulph Mills convicted Thomas Hartnet, 2d Pennsylvania, of deserting to the enemy and sentenced him to be hanged. A general court martial, also at Gulph Mills, sentenced John Morrel, 16th Massachusetts, to death for "desertion from his post while on Centry," handing down its verdict on May 2.[77]

As it turned out, McMarth and Morrel were lucky, for on May 6, to celebrate the announcement of the alliance between France and the United States, Washington pardoned them and ordered their release. Although Hartnet was not mentioned by name, it seems likely that he would have been included in the amnesty issued to all prisoners on May 7.[78]

The final instance of capital punishment at Valley Forge had a different ending. It involved Thomas Shanks, who had been an ensign in the 10th Pennsylvania until he was cashiered, during the autumn of 1777, for stealing a pair of shoes belonging to his captain. Bitter (questions have since been raised regarding his actual guilt of this charge[79]), he offered his services to the British as a spy. He was sent to Valley Forge, with a British sergeant to escort him through the Philadelphia defenses, but the sergeant took advantage of this mission to desert as soon as he had sent Shanks on his way. The sergeant then took a short cut and was waiting with an alerted provost guard when Shanks reached the American camp.[80] Because of the nature of his crime, Shanks was tried on June 2 by a specially convened board of general officers, found guilty, and was hanged on June 4.[81]

There were three recorded cases at Valley Forge in which special steps were taken to humiliate convicted offenders as an indication of the detestation with which their crimes were regarded.

One involved Denham Ford, a commissary in Nathanael Greene's division, convicted by a general court martial on January 1 of stealing 200 dollars. Aside from being sentenced to repay the money, he was to be mounted backwards on a horse, without a saddle, wearing his coat inside out, his hands tied behind him, and drummed out of the army, "never more to return," by all the drums of his division, and his sentence was to be published in the newspapers.[82]

A second was the case of a Lieutenant Frederick Gotthold Enslin, of Colonel William Malcom's "Additional" (unnumbered) Continental Regiment, whom a general court martial of March 10 found guilty of perjury and attempted sodomy. He was sentenced to be "dismiss'd the service with Infamy." Washington, technically exceeding his authority as reviewing officer but moved by his "Abhorrence and Detestation of such Infamous Crimes," added to the sentence by prescribing that Enslin would be drummed out of camp by all the drummers and fifers of the army.[83] Although the sentence did not so specify, a witness reported that Enslin wore his coat turned inside out.[84]

Perhaps the most bizarre punishment of all was one imposed on a Lieutenant Grey, of the 2d Continental Artillery. He was "unanimously sentenced to have his sword broke over his head on the grand parade at guard mounting," to be discharged, and debarred from any future service as an officer; further, the court added a phrase that far exceeded the normal injunction, stating that after this "just, though mild punishment," it would be "esteem'd a crime of the blackest Dye, in any officer or even soldier to associate with him. . . ." So far as the record shows, Grey had been guilty of absence without leave, associating with an enlisted man, and "robbing and infamously steal-ing."[85] Other similar cases brought dishonorable discharges, but with-out the extra features. Although artillery courts martial tended to be somewhat more severe than others, it seems likely that the unrecorded details of Grey's crimes must have been exceptionally heinous.

In addition to these, forty other officers were cashiered, discharged, or dismissed the service. These included eight ensigns, nineteen lieu-tenants, seven captains, two quartermasters, two adjutants, a pay-master, and a lieutenant colonel. However, four of these—an adjutant, two lieutenants, and an ensign—were pardoned or reinstated.

It is interesting to note that, while Washington held intransigent views on gaming, he was much more tolerant of dueling. Ensign John Foster, 6th Pennsylvania, and Lieutenant Martin Shugart, of the Ger-man Regiment[86] (composed of Maryland and Pennsylvania men), were the only individuals tried for issuing challenges to duels; both were sentenced to be cashiered, but both were restored by Washington. And when a Lieutenant White killed a Lieutenant Green (apparently, First Lieutenant John Green, 1st Virginia), of Nathanael Greene's division, in a duel fought in late April,[87] White appears never even to have been brought to trial.

Most of the dismissals were for conduct unbecoming the character of a gentleman, a charge which covered a multitude of sins from being drunk and disorderly to refusal of duty. Disobedience and insubordi-nation accounted for a number of others. Theft, misappropriation, and fraud were also fairly common, the most striking case of this group being that of Lieutenant Colonel Neigal Grey, 12th Pennsyl-vania, who contracted with his men to supplement, for a fee, their inadequate rations, and then defrauded them of the money they had paid.[88]

One individual, Captain Hercules Courtney, of the 4th Continental Artillery, had been convicted by a general court martial on December 29 of behaving in a cowardly manner by abandoning his howitzer at the Battle of Brandywine, but because of his previously good record had been sentenced only to be reprimanded; on February 27, however, he was convicted of neglect of duty, leaving camp while Officer of the Day, and lodging out of camp without permission. This time there was no question of clemency, and he was dismissed the service.[89]

Reprimands were common sentences for lesser offenses. In some cases, the courts prescribed that the reprimand would be delivered privately by the regimental or brigade commander. A number were to be delivered publicly by the regimental, brigade, or divisional commander in the presence of all the officers of that command. Still others were to be published in brigade orders or, in the severest degree of all, in General Orders.

Apparently, reprimands were sometimes resorted to when an individual was technically guilty but the offense was not considered to be especially serious. In any case, they did not have a blighting effect. Major Hadijah Baylies, for example, was sentenced by a general court martial of January 20 to be reprimanded in General Orders for failing to report on time to the grand parade, although he was Brigade Major of the Day; but he was later promoted to lieutenant colonel and, from May, 1782, to December, 1783, served as aide-de-camp to Washington himself.[90]

In addition to officers, some enlisted men were punished by reprimands ordered by courts martial. Sergeant John Henry Leiders wounded a man with his sword, but was let off with a reprimand because of "some alleviating circumstances." Private Samuel Raymond, in an altercation with a lieutenant, threatened the officer with a loaded musket, but the "extreme and unpardonable warmth" shown by the lieutenant "renders the actions of the Prisoner in some measure excusable," so the court awarded only a reprimand by Raymond's troop commander. Although at times the courts martial at Valley Forge appear to have been sticklers for the regulations, they could, as Sergeant Leiders' and Private Raymond's cases illustrate, show understanding of the tensions and frictions which the circumstances encouraged. Another example is that of Forage-Master Adam Gilcrest, who was tried for abusing and threatening to kill an enlisted man; although the court found him guilty, it also stated that "the nature of the insult received by him rendered instant Chastisement necessary," and did not even bother to hand down a sentence.[91]

Perhaps the most surprising case of an enlisted man punished by no more than a reprimand was that of Private Edward Driver, 2d Virginia, who was convicted of mutiny and desertion by a division court martial of Nathanael Greene's division. Driver was involved in a conspiracy between Andrew Welsh, 10th Virginia, and six other members of the 2d Virginia—Thomas Pelton, Robert Edwards, Timothy Dreskill (who had already received 100 lashes for attempted desertion less than a month before), William Cox, Jeremiah Bride, and Richard Johnson —along with Johnson's wife, Mary. Also implicated were John Keyton, 10th Virginia; William McIntire, 2d Virginia; and McIntire's wife, Ann. These individuals were tried by a court martial, but the sentence (which has not been recorded) was disapproved on January 28 as being in excess of what was authorized by the articles of war. On January 29, General Greene approved 100 lashes each for Jeremiah Bride and Mary Johnson (who was also to be drummed out of the army by all the fifes and drums of the division, and appears to have been the ringleader in the plot) and the previously noted reprimand for Driver; John Keyton and William and Ann McIntire were acquitted; the remaining six were sentenced to 100 lashes each, but in their cases the punishment was remitted.[92]

One hundred lashes, normally specified to be "on the bare back, well laid on," appear to have been the usual punishment for desertion, even when desertion was accompanied by additional offenses. For example, on January 22, Private Joseph Tern, 3d Virginia, was sentenced to 100 lashes although he was convicted both of deserting from the provost guard and of releasing a prisoner.[93] As mentioned earlier, John Reily, 2d Virginia, had been hanged less than two weeks earlier for almost the identical offense, the only apparent difference being that Reily had released two prisoners rather than one. All told, twenty-three soldiers were sentenced to 100 lashes, with the floggings being remitted in seven cases (these were the six cases just described and the case of William McMarth, mentioned earlier). Of the sentences of 100 lashes which were carried out, one was for stealing money, one for plundering, and one for striking a lieutenant; all the rest involved desertion, attempted desertion, or inducing others to desert.

Two men, Thomas Coshall and Samuel Burris, both of the 2d Continental Artillery, were sentenced to 500 lashes each for deserting to the enemy, but Washington held that the sentences were illegal and reduced them to 100 lashes, to be administered fifty at a time. In the case of Burris, he added, the man's back was to be well washed with salt water following the second fifty lashes. James Gorden, 2d Virginia, was sentenced on April 8 to receive 300 lashes for deserting, forging a discharge, and then reenlisting, presumably to collect an enlistment bounty, but again Washington reduced the sentence to 100. On June 5, Private William Powell, 2d Rhode Island, was sentenced to 300 lashes, and Matross Edward Connolly, 3d Continental Artillery, to

200, both for offenses similar to Gorden's. Once more, Washington reduced the number of lashes to 100. But on May 13, when Private John Clime, 10th Pennsylvania, had been sentenced to 200 lashes for desertion and attempting to escape to the enemy, the sentence was allowed to stand.[94]

Lesser numbers of lashes were also imposed. Private John Lewis Garew, 2d Rhode Island, received sixty for threatening the lives of a number of officers. Sergeant Helmes, of General Varnum's guard, was reduced to the ranks and given fifty lashes for using insulting language to three officers, trying to hit a lieutenant with a ramrod, and trying to incite troops to mutiny. Private John Conner, 9th Pennsylvania, was acquitted of deserting to the enemy but convicted of taking an oath of allegiance to George III and awarded fifty lashes. Robert Gist, a drummer boy of the 2d Continental Artillery, was awarded fifty lashes for attempting to desert to the enemy; he would have received 100, but was given the lighter sentence "on account of his youth."[95] A conviction on May 3 for desertion brought Private Devall Stripe, of Weedon's brigade, only thirty-nine lashes.[96] And Private Thomas Webb, of Colonel Jackson's regiment (it is not recorded whether this was Colonel Michael Jackson, 8th Massachusetts, or Colonel Henry Jackson, 16th Massachusetts), was sentenced to a mere twenty-five, but his sole crime was "repeatedly getting drunk."[97]

When drunkenness brought on other offenses, it was still viewed with some tolerance. Some time in February, Private William Harris, 9th Pennsylvania, got drunk and quarrelsome. Taking offense at another soldier, named Cameron, Harris knocked him down and threatened to kill him. Private Dennis Kennedy took a hand, also striking and abusing Cameron. Further, Kennedy said that he was going to desert just as soon as he could get some shoes, and while he was at it, he cursed Congress. At that point, Harris and Kennedy were placed into custody, but Harris was still violent and after being confined, lashed out and struck the Corporal of the Guard. Kennedy was sentenced to 100 lashes; but Harris, presumably because he was in his cups, or perhaps because none of his offenses was considered as reprehensible as cursing Congress, got only thirty.[98]

The punishments awarded to civilians caught attempting to trade with or assist the enemy were at least as severe. On January 23, Thomas Butler was sentenced to 250 lashes. On February 4, John Williamson and David Dunn were also awarded sentences of 250 lashes, but Daniel Williamson received only 200. For the floggings of David Dunn and John and Daniel Williamson, Washington directed that a surgeon would be in attendance "to see that the Criminals do not receive more lashes than their strength will bear." Three weeks later, Jacob Cross was found guilty of stealing two calves, taking one into Philadelphia and being in the process of doing the same with the other when arrested; he also received 200 lashes. Rather surprisingly, when Abel Jeans was convicted on March 18 of supplying the enemy with money, trading with them, and buying and passing counterfeit Continental currency, he was sentenced to only 100 lashes, but he was also to be imprisoned for the duration of the war. Three other civilians were at various times sentenced to 100 lashes, but in two of these instances Washington commuted the sentences to one month's "constant fatigue." There were also the cases of Philip Culp and John Bloom, sentenced on April 4 to fifty lashes each (again, Washington remitted the stripes) and to perform hard labor in the public interest for the duration of the British occupation of Pennsylvania unless they chose to enlist in a Continental regiment.[99]

Other punishments of civilians for aid to the enemy took the form of fines (two of 50 pounds—one combined with imprisonment during the British occupation—and two of 100 pounds), the money being used for the benefit of the sick. Aside from those already mentioned, seven other civilians were sentenced to imprisonment while the British remained in the State.

An over-all look at the offenses committed at Valley Forge reveals what might be expected under the circumstances. Many of the cases reflect the semitrained and half-disciplined character of a force just coming into being, the pressures of the situation, and the efforts of authority to instill some standards of professional behavior, particularly in the officer corps. The incidence of courts martial, which might seem excessive, was not unreasonable in view of these considerations, not to mention the lack of any means of handling minor offenses by any other lawful procedures. Many of the punishments awarded seem barbaric by modern standards, but they were consistent with eighteenth-century views of punishment under ordinary law. In terms of military law, especially as compared with normal practices in the Prussian and British armies of the day, they were relatively mild.

Horatio Gates, by Charles Willson Peale

Thomas Mifflin, a James R. Lambdin copy of a
portrait by Gilbert Stuart

V

The People

ENLISTED MEN

LOOKING solely to the designations of the infantry regiments, ten of the thirteen existing states—all but Delaware, South Carolina, and Georgia—supplied units which served at Valley Forge. There were also several infantry regiments manned by soldiers from more than one state, the artillery brigade, and the corps of artificers. In essence, therefore, the encampment must have offered a comprehensive regional representation of the country.

There was also a certain amount of ethnic diversity. Most of the troops, as was to be expected, were of British extraction. However, some of the New England regiments in particular included Indians and Negro soldiers.[1]

The Surgeon of the 1st Connecticut reported the death on January 4 of an Indian soldier,[2] presumably in the same regiment. On January 29, Washington recommended to the Committee on Conference that a unit of 200 or 300 Indians be recruited for scouting and harassing operations,[3] and on March 5, Congress authorized him to enlist up to 400.[4] This plan never materialized, but a group of Oneida Indians, serving as a separate unit, did arrive at Valley Forge on May 14, and others were reported on the way. Because of the new alliance with France, however, Washington no longer saw a need for such unorthodox recruiting, and asked that the prospective arrivals be intercepted and turned back.[5]

The first party of Oneidas, which actually reached Valley Forge, took part under Lafayette in an engagement at Barren Hill (to be described in a later chapter). According to a Connecticut soldier who was present, they numbered "about a hundred." He had mixed feelings about them: he conceded that they were "stout-looking fellows and remarkably neat for that race of mortals," then added, "but they were Indians."[6] Washington seems to have shared this soldier's reservations. As an old frontier fighter, he was apprehensive about introducing into the campaign zone what he called the "irregularities" of Indian-style warfare, and it was with obvious relief that, on June 13, he detailed Ensign Jacob Klock, 1st New York, to supervise the return home of thirty-four of the Oneidas who had tired of soldiering.[7]

As for Negroes, during the fall campaign a Hessian officer had observed that "One sees no [American] regiment in which there are not Negroes in abundance," and a record of August 24, 1778, only some two months after the army left Valley Forge, shows that in seven brigades there were 378 Negro soldiers.[8] Even in the unlikely event that these brigades were at full enlisted strength, this figure would still reflect a proportion of Negro soldiers of something over two per cent. Of course, because a given brigade tended to be made up of regiments from the same state, regional differences would be significant; and although seven brigades would represent upwards of half of Washington's infantry strength, it seems doubtful that the same percentage would have applied across the board.

One Negro soldier known to have served in a Massachusetts regiment at Valley Forge was Salem Poor, a veteran of Bunker Hill who had distinguished himself in that battle.[9] Apparently, a significant number of the members of the two Rhode Island regiments at Valley Forge which were included in General James Varnum's brigade were Negroes;[10] and on January 2, Varnum proposed that a special battalion of Negroes be recruited in Rhode Island to supplement the existing regiments which, because of their reduced strength, he wanted to consolidate.[11] On January 14, and again on February 2, John Laurens suggested to his father (who proved unreceptive) the formation of a corps of up to five thousand slaves, who would be granted their freedom for this service. It is an interesting reflection on young Captain Laurens' perception of soldiering that he saw military service for these men as "a state which would be a proper gradation between abject slavery and perfect liberty."[12]

The bulk of the army, although of European stock, was not necessarily made up primarily of Americans born. Aside from such concrete information as is available (for example, slightly over half of the Pennsylvania Continental soldiers whose places of birth are recorded are shown as being foreign born), the emphasis which was placed on restricting assignment to Washington's Life Guard to native-born Americans[13] suggests that the number of immigrants in the ranks was not inconsiderable. Washington himself, writing on March 17 to President James Bowdoin of Massachusetts, stressed the particular desirability of making increased efforts to enlist men "in whom the ties of Country, kindred, and some times property, are so many securities for their fidelity."[14] Indeed, the number of foreign-born men in the army was sufficiently significant statistically to have noticeable impact on health patterns. Dr. Benjamin Rush reported that "The native Americans were more sickly than the natives of Europe who served in the American Army." [15]

It appears also that there was a considerable age span among the men in the ranks. Rush specifically mentioned young men under twenty as the most susceptible to illness, and observed further that "Men above 30 and 35 years of age were the hardiest soldiers. . . . Perhaps the reason why the natives of Europe were more healthy . . . was, they were more advanced in life." [16]

By the standards of the times, the American soldier—in theory—was the world's most highly paid enlisted man. [17] A Congressional action of May 27, 1778, announced pay rates in conjunction with establishment of the Army's new organizational structure. In infantry units, monthly pay for a private was 6 2/3 dollars; for a corporal, drummer, or fifer, 7 1/3 dollars; for fife majors and drum majors, 9 dollars; and for all sergeants, 10 dollars. The other branches fared better. Cannoneers and dragoon privates drew 8 1/3 dollars; artillery corporals and bombardiers, 9 dollars; artillery sergeants, 10 dollars; artillery fife majors and drum majors, 10 38/90 dollars; and artillery quartermaster sergeants and sergeants major, 11 38/90 dollars. Cavalry corporals, trumpeters, saddlers, and farriers were paid 10 dollars a month; trumpet majors, 11 dollars; and sergeants, 15 dollars. Provost enlisted men received the same pay as cavalrymen, with the ominous addition of men designated as executioners, who were paid 10 dollars a month. Engineer soldiers were paid at the rates prescribed for artillerymen. [18]

In practice, however, inflation had robbed the money of most of its value; and in any case, the pay was usually long in arrears.

On January 3, a General Order announced that, in recognition of the hardship the army would undergo by spending the winter in huts, Congress had resolved that the officers and men who continued in the service would be granted an extra month's pay. But the resolution was ambiguous. On January 9, Washington postponed action in compiling the rosters for this payment, and on the same day wrote to President Laurens, asking clarification. Was the payment to be made only to those present at Valley Forge on the day Congress passed the resolution? If so, what about loyal soldiers who happened to be temporarily absent on furlough, or sick in hospital, or on detached duty? Evidently, the whole matter had become a sore subject, threatening to sow "great disgust and uneasiness" in the army, and Washington went on to say rather testily that "For my part, tho' the Resolves were founded in principles of generosity, were intended to reward merit and promote the service, from the difficulties attending the execution,

I wish they had never been made, especially, as I believe, Officers and Men would in a little time have been tolerably well reconciled in their Quarters." Not until February 15 was it possible to announce a ruling: all officers and men in camp on December 29, and all who had since joined the army there, would be eligible to receive the extra pay. The actual money, however, was not paid to the troops until March 11.[19]

Even the regular pay situation was bad. As of February 3, the average arrears of pay for the soldiers at Valley Forge was three months, with many having gone unpaid for four or five months, and some even longer. A week later, money was available to pay the troops the sums due them for the previous November. There appears to have been some temporary improvement, for December and January pay was issued in the latter part of February. But not until the first week of June were the troops paid for February and March.[20]

This was no trifling matter, as it impacted directly on the attitude and morale of the troops. On January 29, Washington patiently explained to the Committee on Conference that

> Besides feeding and cloathing a soldier well, nothing is of greater importance than paying him with punctuality; and it is perhaps more essential in our army, than in any other, because our Men are worse supplied and more necessitous; and the notions of implicit subordination, not being as yet, sufficiently ingrafted among them, they are more apt to reason upon their rights and readier to manifest their sensibility of any thing, that has the appearance of injustice to them; in which light they consider their being kept out of their pay, after it is due.[21]

Certainly, there was ample incentive for the men to rebel, and a number of Washington's statements and actions show that he seriously anticipated a mutiny. Writing to the President of Congress on December 23, in apparent reference to the chant of "No meat, no meat" which echoed through the camp on December 21, he said that "I was . . . convinced, that . . . a dangerous Mutiny begun the Night before, and [which] with difficulty was suppressed by the spirited exertion's of some officers was still much to be apprehended. . . ." Again, on February 14, he asserted to General Sullivan that "The Soldiers have been with great difficulty prevented from Mutiny for want of Victuals. . . ." Two days later, to Governor George Clinton of New York, he stated that "Strong symptoms . . . of discontent have appeared in particular instances; and nothing but the most active efforts every where can long avert so shocking a catastrophe [as a general mutiny and dispersion]."[22]

It may also be significant that, when large groups of soldiers assembled in impromptu gatherings, even for what turned out to be quite innocuous purposes, Washington went to considerable lengths to avoid confrontations with them. Later chapters will describe such episodes on Washington's birthday and during a potentially boisterous May Day celebration. On the other hand, when a near-riot between Virginia and Massachusetts regiments is said to have occurred on St. Patrick's Day, demanding authoritative intervention, he is described as being prompt and vigorous in dealing with it by forceful personal leadership. It was not that Washington was reluctant to face the men; rather, whenever possible, he wanted to avoid the possibility of becoming part of a situation which might escalate beyond a level of insubordination which he could officially ignore.

As events proved, the fundamental dedication of the bulk of the soldiers at Valley Forge was greater than many of their superiors appreciated. Of course, there was some surliness, continuing well through the winter, but this did not reflect a basic erosion of discipline. Pierre Duponceau, Steuben's secretary, writing of events in March, said that "I remember seeing the soldiers popping their heads out of their miserable huts, and calling out in an undertone, 'No bread, no soldier!' "[23] And as late as March 20, a letter from Washington to General Cadwalader said that "notwithstanding and contrary to my expectations we have been able to keep the Soldiers from Mutiny or dispersion, although . . . they have encountered enough to occasion one or the other of these in most Armies. . . ."[24]

To a degree, of course, the sheer requirements of survival kept the men too occupied to cause trouble, and at times hunger must have kept them too debilitated. Reference has been made to the massive tasks of erecting the huts, constructing the bridge and the fortifications, cutting and hauling firewood, trying to find provisions, and seeing (admittedly, not too energetically) to the police of the camp area. In addition, there were formations to be stood, tours manning pickets and the eleven guard posts—stints at the latter were reduced to a maximum of forty-eight hours only by a General Order of May 3[25]— and occasional forays against roving British detachments. There was also, particularly after Steuben began his training program, an intensive daily schedule of drill.

On February 8, whatever the schedule had been was changed so that from then on the drums would beat reveille at dawn, the "troop" (the beginning of all duty details) at 8 A.M., retreat at sunset, and "taptoo" at 9 P.M. The drummers were to begin beating the calls at the right of the front line; this would be answered along the length of that line, then through the second line and the artillery brigade, and finally through the Reserve. When the call was complete, the drummers would beat three rolls, following the same sequence. Finally, all the drums of the army, "at the heads of their respective Corps," would go through "the regular beat," ceasing upon the right as a signal for all the drumming to halt. This schedule was changed, effective March 30, so that the "troop" would be beaten half an hour earlier, with the guard assembling on the Grand Parade by 8 A.M. so as to practice its movements before guard mount. It was changed again on May 3: drill was to be carried out from 6 A.M. to 8 A.M., and from 5 P.M. to 6 P.M. This, in turn, required changing the prescribed hours for drummers' practice; these were now to be during the hour preceding the new times scheduled for drill. In an obvious response to confusion and disturbance which must have been taking place, the order continued to warn sternly that

> Any drummer that shall be found practicing at any other . . .
> time . . . shall be severely punished. The Adjutants of the
> several Regiments are to pay particular Attention to this or-
> der, as they will be answerable for the Execution of it. . . .
> If every Drummer is allowed to beat at his pleasure, . . . it
> will be impossible to distinguish whether they are beating
> for their own pleasure or for a signal to the Troops.[26]

But the Valley Forge soldier's life was not exclusively one of fatigues, deprivations, and the noise of drums. Soon after the army went into winter quarters, Washington prepared a list of instructions to regimental commanders. Included were these directives:

> Let Vice and immorality of every kind be discouraged as
> much as possible . . . , and see . . . that the Men regularly
> attend divine Worship. Gaming of every kind is expressly
> forbid as the foundation of evil. . . . Games of exercise, for
> amusement, may not only be allowed of, but Incouraged.[27]

Religious activity was an important part of the men's civilian experience, and continued to be so in the army. However, the lack of buildings large enough for services and the lack of clothes to permit the men to endure protracted periods of inactivity listening to sermons outdoors inhibited religious activities during the winter. For this reason, it appears that a number of the chaplains left the army until spring brought better weather.[28] Some, however, remained, and all of them united in protesting Nathanael Greene's appointment of John Murray, a Universalist, as chaplain of a Rhode Island regiment; but when the protest was ignored, the clergymen subsided.[29] By resolution of Congress, strongly endorsed by Washington, April 22 was designated as a day of fasting, humiliation, and prayer; no duty was to be performed and regimental chaplains were directed to "prepare discourses suitable to the occasion." On May 2, orders were issued that divine services be held at 11 A.M. every Sunday in each brigade to which a chaplain was assigned; troops whose organizations had no chaplains were to "attend the places of worship nearest them." Washington went on to exhort the army that "While we are zealously performing the duties of good Citizens and soldiers we certainly ought not to be inattentive to the higher duties of Religion. To the distinguished Character of Patriot, it should be our highest Glory to add the more distinguished Character of Christian." At the same time, he prohibited any further fatigue duties on Sundays.[30]

As for "games of exercise, for amusement," it is doubtful that during the hard, cold days of the winter the men had either inclination or spare energy for athletics. Warmer weather brought a change, however, and there were various games. One, a form of bowls played with cannon balls, was called "long bullets."[31] Another, called "base," appears to have been a version of rounders, the ancestor of baseball. Still a third was cricket. Occasionally, there was a rude practical joke, as when "some Rogueish chaps tied a sheaf of straw" to the tail of a horse belonging to the Quartermaster of General William Maxwell's brigade. Setting the straw afire, they turned the terrified beast loose to run. Understandably, this "very much offended" the Brigade Quartermaster, who made a formal complaint to Maxwell.[32] There is no record, however, of the men responsible being brought to book.

Of what might be called "social life" for the enlisted men, there was almost none. Contact with local civilian families was severely limited by the restrictions on movement of soldiers outside the camp. During the autumn, a considerable number of women had accompanied the army as shown by the repeated General Orders which attempted to encourage them to leave or to restrict their taking up space in the baggage wagons. It seems probable that most of them did leave by the time the army reached Valley Forge, but some of them continued to be a problem.

On February 4, Washington issued an order observing that "The most pernicious consequences having arisen from suffering persons, women in particular to pass and repass from Philadelphia to camp under Pretence of coming out to visit Friends in the Army and returning with necessaries to their families, but really with an intent to intice the soldiers to desert," and directing that "All officers are desired to exert their utmost endeavors to prevent such interviews in future by forbidding the soldiers under the severest penalties from having any communication with such persons and by ordering them when found in camp to be immediately turned out of it."[33]

Perhaps this order was an outgrowth of the previously mentioned experience with Mary Johnson and Ann McIntire, whose case had been dealt with less than a week earlier.

There are a few other references to women with the troops at Valley Forge. On March 6, an officer was acquitted of encouraging a soldier's wife to sell liquor without permission. As stated earlier, Washington sought at the end of May to employ "Women of the Army" as nurses, and in the same order directed that all officers "pay the strictest Attention that no Women be suffered on any Pretence to get into the Waggons of the Army on the march." Courts martial records of June 2 and June 8 mention the presence on May 15 of "Women of bad reputation" in the hut of Sergeant Thomas Howcroft, 10th Pennsylvania, and also make reference to the presence of the sergeant's family.[34] Even earlier, on April 26, a regimental surgeon ungallantly reported in verse on some of the women inhabiting the camp, observing that

> What! though there are, in rags, in crape, some beings
>   here in female shape,
> In whom may still be found some traces of former beauty
>   in their faces,
> Yet now so far from being nice, they boast of every
>   barefaced vice.
> Shame to their sex! 'Tis not in these one e'er beholds
>   those charms that please.[35]

From the dates of these references, it would appear that many of the women came or returned to Valley Forge only after the winter was over. Some, however, evidently endured through the winter with the troops. This is said to have been particularly true of the wives of Pennsylvania soldiers, who were reasonably near to their homes.[36] There were also women who were, in effect, authorized members of specific organizations. Mrs. Mary Geyer, serving as a laundress on the regimental strength of the 13th Pennsylvania, had accompanied her husband, Peter, and her eleven-year-old son, John, when they enlisted for twenty-one months in the spring of 1776. Peter, a rifleman, and John, a drummer, were wounded at the Battle of Germantown—Peter being permanently disabled—but all three remained with the army until their enlistments were completed and Peter and John were discharged at Valley Forge[37] on January 1, 1778. Mary, with John helping, stayed on through the encampment, continuing to work as a laundress.[38] A somewhat similar case of another woman who stayed with the army as a laundress is that of a Mrs. Milliner, who remained at Valley Forge to care for her young son, Alexander, who was also a drummer boy.[39]

In general, regarding the men in the ranks at Valley Forge, what little information that is available tends to concentrate on official matters such as drill schedules, fatigue details, records of punishments, and recitations of shortages. As for the specifics of daily life, the picture is indistinct at best. It seems clear, though, that from the soldier's viewpoint the six months at Valley Forge must have been a period of hard work, hardship, and dull, bleak boredom. Most Americans of the time led a relatively isolated and uneventful existence, relieved only by rare and simple breaks in routine. Even by those standards, however, the army's period in winter quarters was exceptionally drab.

Under the circumstances, it is astonishing that the men's spirits remained as high as they did. Yet there is no question that they did indeed remain high. The central thrust of the recorded observations of Washington, the other senior officers, and the Committee on Conference is amazement and admiration at the patience, endurance, and fidelity of the troops.

In spite of all the hardships, morale in the ranks remained strong enough to hold the army together. The fact that this was so seems to stem largely from two fundamental sources. One was widespread and profound esteem for Washington and trust in his leadership. The other was the men's devotion to the cause they served. Every recorded fact makes it indisputably obvious that one of the most striking characteristics of the American soldier at Valley Forge was that he was a dedicated man, aware of the issues at stake, determined to uphold them, and unshakably confident of the final outcome.

THE OFFICERS

Among the officers, the situation as regards morale was in a number of respects considerably different. This is hardly surprising, for other than those holding the highest ranks, the officers at Valley Forge were in many ways worse off than their men. It has been pointed out that more was demanded of them, but proportionally less by far was given in return.

Whereas an enlisted soldier was at least theoretically entitled to rations, clothing, and equipment, officers had to follow the European custom of providing their needs from their own pockets. But while the European system took this into account in establishing pay rates, the American system did not. Congress was enamored of the ideal of egalitarianism, and had adopted the concept of "leveling" to reduce or eliminate distinctions of status. To this end, the rates Congress authorized provided relatively marginal differences in pay from one rank to the next. Thus, while the American soldier's prescribed pay—entirely apart from the bounties offered for enlistment—was substantially higher than that of the Englishman or Hessian he fought, the American officer's pay was only a fraction of what his British counterpart drew. For example, a captain of Continentals was entitled to about a third as much as his British opposite number; and even when officers' pay and allowances were increased by a third on May 27, 1778, the American was still receiving only about half what was paid a British officer of the same rank.[40]

Consequently, the failure to pay on schedule and the depreciation of money hit the officers especially hard. Making their situation worse was the fact that the characteristics of maturity and civilian standing which led to individuals being commissioned as officers in the first place meant that they were more likely than the soldiers as a whole to have heavy responsibilities at home.

The diary of one officer at Valley Forge states the problem explicitly. Writing on December 28 of officers' difficulties, he said that "Their Wages will not by considerable, purchase a few Comfortables here in Camp, & maintain their families at home. . . . What then have they to purchase Cloaths and other necessaries with?" He went on to say that "The present Circumstances of the Soldier is better by far than the Officers—for the family of the Soldier is provided for at the public expence . . . but the Officer's family, are obliged . . . to pay [for necessities] . . . at the most exorbitant rates. . . ." For those blessed with private incomes, the situation was endurable, although only at the jeopardy of their future financial security, but by no means all were so fortunately situated. The diary continues, saying that

> . . . many of them who depend entirely on their Money [military pay], cannot procure half the material comforts that are wanted in a family. This produces continual letters of complaint from home. When the Officer . . . finds a letter directed to him from his Wife, fill'd with the most heart aching tender Complaints, a Woman is capable of writing . . . concluding

with expressions bordering on despair, of procuring a suffi-
ciency of food . . . [,] that her money is of very little consequence to her—that she begs of him to consider that Charity
begins at home . . . who would not be disheartened from per-
severing in the best of Causes . . . ?[41]

Although Washington himself drew no salary, being paid only for
his expenses, he was deeply sympathetic. On January 29, he recommended that Congress adopt a measure which would entitle ex-officers
after the war to half pay for life. It would cost nothing for the time
being, as he said, but it

> . . . would not only dispel the [officers'] apprehension of
> personal distress, at the termination of the war, from having
> thrown themselves out of professions and employments, they
> might not have it in their power to resume; but would in great
> degree, relieve the painful anticipation, of leaving their
> Widows and Orphans, a burthen on the charity of their
> country, should it be their lot to fall in its defence.[42]

Throughout the winter, he continued to press for this program.
However, it met severe obstacles. Congress was dilatory at best, but
in this case there was strong opposition, especially from the New
England delegations, led by Massachusetts. Repeatedly, Washington
emphasized the consequences of failure to provide adequately for the
officers. Good officers by the score were resigning their commissions.
Those who remained, he was writing as late as April 10, were growing
increasingly indifferent to their responsibilities, and he cited the number of officers who had been cashiered for dereliction of duty: ". . .
Untill Officers consider their Commissions in an honorable, and [ma-
terially] interested point of view, and are afraid to endanger them by
negligence or inattention, . . . no order, regularity, or care, either of
the Men, or Public property, will prevail." In sum, without some
material incentive being provided, "your Officers will moulder to
nothing, or be composed of low and illiterate men void of capacity
for this, or any other business."[43]

Nevertheless, it was not until May 18 that announcement was made
that Congress had approved a half-pay measure. Even then, Massachusetts had been able to block full adoption, and what resulted was
a program which provided for all officers who remained in the service
for the duration of the war half pay for seven years thereafter, or until
the officer's death, if that occurred sooner. A general officer's payment,
moreover, was to be limited to that of a colonel.[44]

Even allowing for the differences in the value of money, and even
after the new pay scales were established on May 27, the salaries were

hardly generous. Because of the superior technical skills required, artillery officers drew the highest monthly rates, ranging from 100 dollars for a colonel to 33 1/3 dollars for a second lieutenant. Cavalry pay, due to the extra costs of maintaining mounts, ran from the 93 3/4 dollars of a colonel to the 26 2/3 dollars of a cornet (cavalry second lieutenant). An infantry colonel got only seventy-five dollars a month, and an ensign (infantry second lieutenant) twenty.[45] In addition, in lieu of the extra rations previously authorized in theory, on June 2 officers were granted a ration allowance, beginning at ten dollars a month for lieutenants, ensigns, and cornets, and increasing by ten-dollar increments by grade to the colonels' fifty dollars a month.[46] On June 9, Congress directed that for the rations to which the officers had been previously entitled and had not received between January 1 and June 1, reimbursement would be paid at the rate of one-third of a dollar per day.[47]

When the army first reached Valley Forge, however, all this was months in the future. It is small wonder, therefore, that the encampment had hardly begun when there was a landslide of applications for leave, accompanied by a considerable amount of unauthorized absence. On December 22, Washington felt compelled to order that only division commanders could grant leaves to subaltern officers, and he himself would approve all leaves for captains and above. On December 27, he issued a General Order stating that

> Notwithstanding the orders repeatedly given, for calling the absent officers to camp, ... many are still scattered about the Country, mispending their time, to the prejudice of the service, and injury of those officers who remain and attend their duty in camp. ... Such as are absent without leave ... , or having had such leave remain unnecessarily absent, are to be immediately notified to return to camp without delay on pain of being suspended or cashiered.

Less than a week later, on January 2, he directed that any leave application reaching him must be accompanied by a division commander's certificate recommending approval, and that such certificates should be granted only when the leave could be approved "without Injury to the Service." His two great concerns were to carry out the work of establishing the winter quarters and to take advantage of the opportunity which "the leisure of a fixed Camp will afford" to improve the training of the troops and the professional competence of the officers.[48]

But the problem continued. On February 9, Washington was writing that "It is a matter of no small grief to me, to find such an unconquerable desire in the Officers of this Army to be absent from Camp. . . ." On March 15 he said that "A great number of Officers are now absent, and many more are pressing for the same purpose," and less than a week later, "the daily applications for . . . furloughs distresses me beyond measure."[49] Furthermore, those officers who obtained leaves found numerous excuses to overstay them, and repeated orders had to be sent to individuals to return.

It was by no means merely the junior officers who were involved. On December 27, Washington refused permission to Anthony Wayne to leave camp until the huts were all built; as of January 9, he was urging Generals Learned and Glover to return from leave (Learned never came back, and Washington was still pleading with Glover to return, after one extension, as late as March 15) ; General Muhlenberg was on leave in February, and Generals Woodford and Scott had made application; General Huntington was absent in April. Understandably, Washington felt obliged to discourage a request from General Weedon and to refuse outright one from General Sullivan and, later, another from General Varnum. This last, however, was couched in such courtly language that Varnum could hardly have felt resentment. After reviewing the problems, Washington concluded with the hope that ". . . you will . . . endeavour to conciliate your happiness with the public Interest and the good of the Service." At one time in February there were only three major generals in camp, several brigades were without brigadiers, and many regiments had no officer present above the rank of captain. It is no wonder that, in the absence of so many senior officers, Washington complained ruefully that he must carry out alone all the tasks of reorganizing the army, supervising the training of the troops, "and perform the part of a Brigadier, a Colonel, &ca. . . ."[50]

Not all requests were rejected as graciously as General Varnum's. When Washington considered that the application was unjustified, he could be acid. Colonel William Malcom, whose regiment had not been activated until the previous April, and had spent most of its service not far from home, was told that ". . . you cannot be surprised that I disapproved your application," which had been received with "some degree of displeasure." Washington went on to say that "It has been a custom with several Officers to resign of late when Furloughs could not be granted them. . . . This practice you seem to wish to pursue; I therefore inform you, However anxious I might have been before for your continuance in the Army, that if you can obtain liberty from

Congress to resign, to whom it will be necessary to apply, that you will meet with no difficulty from me."[51] It is not surprising that, thus caustically admonished, Colonel Malcom abandoned his threat to leave the army.

Resignations, whether or not Washington raised difficulties, were legion. On December 28, an officer claimed that "Yesterday upwards of fifty Officers in Gen¹ Greene's Division resigned their Commissions. Six or Seven of our Regiment [1st Connecticut Continentals] are doing the like today." The next day he noted that "So much talk about discharges among the Officers, and so many are discharged, his Excellency [Washington] lately expressed his fears of being left Alone with Soldiers only."[52]

In several instances, where outstanding men were involved, Washington did not hesitate to plead personally for them to reconsider, but by February 18 he was saying that "The spirit of resigning, which is now become almost epidemical, is truely painful and alarming." Further, so many officers who had gone on leave had taken to sending in resignations from home that on April 4 Washington threatened that any who tried to leave the service without at least returning to Valley Forge to clear their accounts "may depend upon being dealt with in a very disagreeable manner."[53]

But the situation grew no better. On April 21, Washington noted that the trend, which "has been long at an alarming height, . . . increases daily," and on April 30 he wrote to President Laurens that

> Day after day, and hour after hour produces resignations; if they were confined to bad Officers, or to those of little or no character, they would be of no consequence. But it is painful to see men . . . who have rendered great Services . . . and who are still . . . most materially wanted, leaving the Army, on acct. of the distresses of their family. . . .[54]

To Washington's frequently expressed chagrin, resignations were highest among the Virginia officers. By March 24, he noted that "In the Virginia line only, not less than Six Colonels as good as any in the Service" had resigned; by April 21, fully ninety Virginia officers of all grades had given up their commissions; "the same conduct has prevailed among the other States," Washington noted, "though not yet to so considerable a degree. . . ."[55]

Apart from the vital questions of pay and family problems, officer morale was also depressed by a number of other factors. One of these stemmed from the loss of security of their appointments. Virtually all regiments were far below adequate manning levels in enlisted strength but most had approximately full complements of officers. The prospect of reorganization of the army, which was obviously necessary, meant that when regiments were consolidated, many officers would become supernumerary, being "deranged," in the parlance of the times.

Another factor adversely affecting officer morale was the lack of any clear or equitable system of appointment and promotion.

Within regiments, with prescribed numbers of ranks, the problem of appointment was not serious. Unfortunately, however, Congress had been lavish in bestowing high military rank on commissaries and other officials who, although performing important tasks, were not officers of the army. Noting this, as well as other appointments made without regard to the existence of specific assignments, Washington wrote on January 29 that "No error can be more pernicious than that of dealing out rank with too prodigal a hand." In addition, when a vacancy occurred within a regiment, there were instances when efforts were made to claim it by officers commissioned as it were "at large" through what Washington called "irregular promotions." Predictably, the officers in the regiment thought that any vacancy should be filled by promotion from among themselves. Such cases had caused "uneasiness, discord and perplexity in this Army," resulting in "numerous bickerings and resignations," and had "occasioned infinite trouble and vexation."[56]

In the absence of established regulations on the subject, the different sources of appointment and the complications injected by the fact that some officers had not had continuous service brought on a number of serious disputes over seniority. Given the delicate sense of "honor" demanded of the eighteenth-century gentleman, the result was that whoever lost out in such a dispute usually felt obliged to resign rather than serve under one whom, regardless of the tribunal rendering the judgment, he considered his military "inferior." In one case, such a dispute involved no fewer than four brigadier generals, two of whom threatened to leave the service if their contention was not upheld. In view of the shortage of proven senior officers, this was no matter to be taken lightly.

The principals were Generals William Woodford, Peter Muhlenberg, Charles Scott, and George Weedon, all of Virginia. When they had all been colonels, Woodford had been the senior, but he had resigned. Later, he had reentered the army as a brigadier, on the same date that Muhlenberg was promoted to that rank and less than a week before Weedon's promotion. Because of their continuous service, Muhlenberg and Weedon claimed that they, and Scott as well (he had been promoted a few weeks later), should rank ahead of

Woodford; but Woodford argued that he should take precedence among the Virginia brigadiers on the basis of his former seniority as a colonel.[57] In December, the question was referred to Congress, which held that the matter was outside its competence. Washington therefore decided to convene a board of general officers to consider it, but the lack of generals at Valley Forge delayed consideration until March 4. By March 15, the board had voted unanimously in favor of Woodford's claim, but had been unwilling to take a final stand without referring the matter again to Congress. Some time within the next two weeks, Congress ruled in favor of Woodford.[58] Weedon eventually resigned. Muhlenberg submitted his resignation, arguing that the decision had reflected on his performance by demoting him, in effect,[59] and that in any case Woodford had obtained the ruling by lobbying with friends in Congress. Patiently, Washington reasoned with the offended brigadier, asking him to withdraw his resignation,[60] and Muhlenberg ultimately relented.

Similar disputes arose among officers of lesser rank.

For example, a protest by captains of the Pennsylvania Line required a board to be convened on February 16 to rule on the competing claims of Michael Ryan and James Grier to be major, 10th Pennsylvania. Grier, the regiment's senior captain, had been wounded at the Battle of Brandywine and was absent, convalescing, when the vacancy occurred as the result of the promotion and transfer of Major Caleb North. Ryan, who was brigade major of Anthony Wayne's brigade, claimed the position by virtue of seniority, but was challenged on the grounds that his seniority as a staff officer did not apply within a regiment. After several sessions, the board upheld Grier, but Ryan was still protesting as late as April 10, when Washington himself had to intervene to silence him.[61]

Another controversy arose over a foreign volunteer, Chevalier Thomas Antoine Mauduit du Plessis. On January 29, Washington asked Congress to recognize Du Plessis' gallant conduct during the recent campaign with a brevet (honorary) promotion to lieutenant colonel, stating that, being only a brevet which would not affect regimental seniority, this "will not have the inconvenience of occasioning any dissatisfaction in the Corps to which he belongs." Congress acted on the request, but proceeded to assign Du Plessis to the artillery brigade, where he took position according to his brevet rank. The resentful artillery officers formed a committee of a colonel and three captains to protest. Washington repeatedly argued that brevet rank did not affect the other officers' seniority, but the committee as often maintained that it did. As the artillerymen now challenged whether Du Plessis had actually performed the acts leading to his brevet, Du Plessis himself pushed his claim, and the matter had to be referred to a board of general officers; but the non-availability of key witnesses[62] kept the question from ever being settled, and Du Plessis finally resigned the following autumn.

Still other controversies arose when a captain who was a prisoner of war was promoted to a vacant majority (Washington ruled in his favor) and when a Major John Popkins, 3d Artillery, was promoted to lieutenant colonel in his own regiment although Major Thomas Forrest, 4th Artillery, was senior to him. Washington argued that promotion was regimental, so Forrest had no basis for complaint, but the question was taken up by the artillery officers' committee, and was not finally settled until a board reached a ruling in favor of Popkins on the following September 15.[63]

Truly, as one officer at Valley Forge observed, "Rank & Precedence make a good deal of disturbance & confusion in the American Army."[64] However, while it would be easy to do so, it would be wrong to write these controversies off to pettiness. To a degree, of course, they stemmed from vanity and exaggerated notions of "honor." More fundamentally, however, they were caused by the lack of any clear-cut system for appointing and promoting officers. (In desperation, Washington wrote on May 29 concerning procedures on this subject that "My earnest wish is that something, I do not care what, may be fixed and the regulations compleated...."[65]) The disputes were important because of their impact on morale. And in one sense, they were a healthy sign that since at least some of the officers valued their commissions, the army was moving—however slowly—toward a point where Washington's misgivings about deterioration of quality through indifference would lose their justification.

There were other sources of quarrels as well. It was a contentious and litigious age, and the frictions and tensions of the situation gave extra cause for resentments and fancied slights. On March 22, Washington wrote that ". . . nothing gives me more pain than the frequency of . . . difference of various kinds . . . among a set of Men . . . who ought rather to cultivate harmony than break out into dissentions upon almost every occasion that offers." Two weeks later he was again exhorting his officers that he "wishes the Officers of his Army to consider themselves as a band of brothers . . . and that they would settle all personal disputes . . . in an amicable manner, ever being cautious not to trouble Courts Martial or the General with private dissentions or add papers to the public files which may hereafter reflect disgrace upon themselves and the Army."[66]

But not all the officers at Valley Forge were preoccupied with bickering and disputes. They had routine duty as officers of the day, at guard mount, on picket, and taking part in the frequent patrolling toward Philadelphia. From the record, they certainly must have spent a great deal of time sitting as members of courts martial. After Steuben's training program began, the junior officers especially were increasingly involved in the detailed supervision of the troops. In addition, there was the matter of improving their own knowledge. At the outset, Washington had pointed out that "As War is a science, . . . a great deal of useful knowledge and Instruction [is] to be drawn from Books," and had told the regimental commanders that "you are to cause your Officers to devote some part of their time to reading Military Authors. . . ."[67]

How religiously this particular directive was observed may be questioned, and certainly there were instances of ineptitude. At one stage, excessive zeal seems to have led to some minor disasters, for on March 26 a General Order prohibited officers from leading out unauthorized parties, as "many officers have been captivated by their own folly and carelessness. . . ."[68]

The lieutenants and ensigns in particular fully shared the men's hardships and deprivations and, as an observer noted, demonstrated similar dedication and endurance.[69] They also shared the hazards of disease and exposure. A sufficient number of officers died for funerals to become a problem, and on April 12 a General Order was issued directing that "The Funeral Honors at the Interment of Officers are for the future to be confined to a solemn Procession . . . in number suitable to the rank of the deceased with Revers'd Arms; Firing [of salutes] on those occasions . . . is to be abolished."[70]

Nor were the discomforts and sacrifices confined solely to subalterns. As noted earlier, most of the generals rented nearby houses, but two at least—Greene[71] and Steuben[72]—were housed for a good part of the time in huts.

There were some attempts to provide amenities. In the 13th Pennsylvania, for example, there were what amounted to scheduled social activities. A junior officer of that unit reported that on January 14

> At the request of Colonel [Walter] Stewart, the officers of the regiment were summoned to dine with him, where we spent the day in civil jolity. In this manner several days were spent, passing by a rotation from the senior to the junior

officers. Thus and in many other desirable enjoyments we spent some part of the Winter . . . , making ourselves as happy as circumstances would possibly admit. While confined to the camp, we passed many hours in recreation, viewing the environs thereof. . . .

But "viewing the environs" had a purpose other than mere amusement, for the account goes on to say that in these walks the officers "surveyed the most advantageous posts in case of an attack."[73]

Another social activity stemmed from the custom whereby the field and general officers of the day dined with Washington. A change had to be made, however, when it was found that this practice hampered these officers in making their rounds; thereafter, the officers of the day dined with Washington on the day following their duty tours.[74]

Another pastime for some was instituted early in February. "Some Gentlemen of the camp Hospital being desirous of improving in the accomplishment of dancing," it was announced, "Mr. John Trotter has agreed to open a school for their accommodation." Mr. Trotter, with long experience as a dancing master in New York, was "about" fifty-eight years old; but he was "a small, genteel, well-proportioned man, every limb and joint proclaiming that he is formed for his profession, and the ease and grace with which he moves on the floor, evince, that . . . he has lost none of his agility by age."[75]

There were other indications of polite society as well. In January, General Nathanael Greene's wife, Catherine, arrived at Valley Forge. Since she spoke some French, she was especially popular with the European officers.[76] Martha Washington had reached camp by February 10.[77] Apparently she and Mrs. Greene did not have a great deal in common, for Elias Boudinot, the American commissioner for the exchange of prisoners, noted that she was "almost a mope for want of a female companion" and sent for his own wife to keep her company.[78] General Lord Stirling's wife, with their daughter, Lady Kitty, was also in camp,[79] as was Rebecca Biddle, whose husband was Colonel Clement Biddle, the Forage-Master General.[80] Lucy Knox, wife of General Henry Knox, did not arrive until May 20, escorted by General Benedict Arnold, who was still recuperating from the wound received during the Saratoga campaign. She made up for her late arrival, however, by remaining with the army throughout the rest of the war.[81] Mrs. Greene, on the other hand, had started home by May 25,[82] and Mrs. Washington followed soon after, leaving on June 9.[83] Although no references to other women survive, it seems highly probable that some of the less senior officers also brought their wives to Valley Forge for visits of varying lengths. General De Kalb speaks of fifteen hundred officers and their ladies attending the celebration of the French alliance on May 6,[84] and while the ladies would have been greatly outnumbered, the statement seems to imply a greater number of them than the seven whose names have been mentioned.

The ladies' presence brought some upsurge in dinners and receptions, although camp life was not without its inconveniences for the women. Mrs. Greene lived for a time in a hut, and a drummer boy reported many years later that Martha Washington had used thorns instead of pins on her clothes.[85] But while they were there, the women added an element of civility that had previously been lacking. Some of them formed acquaintances with ladies of the surrounding area, and visits were exchanged.[86] It is probable that they also furnished the stimulus which resulted in a number of relatively elaborate entertainments. On April 15, for example, some of the officers and ladies joined forces to stage a play for an audience which jammed the "Bake House,"[87] and on May 11, Joseph Addison's play, *Cato,* was presented.[88]

As for the officers' more active recreations, there are records showing that as spring wore on, they played "base" as well as cricket, which was also called "wicket." Indeed, one day early in May, after dining with General Knox, Washington himself took a bat to join in a cricket match with the artillery officers.[89]

The most significant consideration regarding the officers at Valley Forge, however, is that, while for both officers and men it was a time of training, for the officers it was also a time of screening and weeding out. The numerous dismissals had gone far to eliminate from the army those who were deficient in character or ability or responsibility; the resignations had eliminated many who lacked the determination to persist, or who genuinely felt that the claims of their families had to be given priority over the claims of the service; the half-pay measure had provided a material incentive; and the example and instruction of Steuben had opened entirely new conceptual horizons regarding the scope of an officer's duty. Those who remained, therefore, were well on the way to becoming the nucleus of the corps of dedicated, proficient, and responsible officers whose role was to be crucial to the ultimate success of the war.

THE COMMANDER-IN-CHIEF

In a number of significant respects, the story of the army at Valley Forge is essentially the story of George Washington. Previous chapters have shown the comprehensive nature of his personal involvement in every aspect of the army's existence, from broad policy to the most minute details. He had to deal not only with the troops at Valley Forge, but also with the detachments at Wilmington, Delaware, and Trenton, New Jersey, and the other commands in the Hudson Valley and in New England; not only with the army but with the Board of War, the Congress, and the governing bodies of the several states. His concerns included all aspects of supply, recruitment, reorganization, training, discipline, health, tactical activities, and strategic and diplomatic planning.

It is not that Washington in any way sought to dominate. The fact was, however, that there was no one able or available to share his burdens. In a day when the military staff was just beginning to evolve, the lack of qualified subordinates meant that even a rudimentary staff was essentially lacking. To a large extent, Washington's staff consisted only of aides and military secretaries, not of officers capable of being placed in charge of agencies carrying out broad functions. In addition, the line officers were limited in administrative capability, and as has been pointed out, many of those who were in key positions were absent for protracted periods.

All this imposed a heavy load, confining Washington to headquarters much more than could have suited a man of his preference for outdoor, physical activity. The Isaac Potts house, where Washington lived and worked, was certainly more comfortable than a tent or a hut, but Washington still found it desirable to have a log structure built nearby to serve as a dining room.[90] With the five senior officers of the day and his nine aides, a minimum of fourteen normally dined with Washington. Martha's arrival increased the number; and after late February, according to Captain Duponceau, Steuben and his three aides ate at Washington's table "twice or thrice a week."[91] Thus, even with the extra room, meals must have been crowded affairs. For a considerable period, moreover, Washington's discomfort was increased by the absence of his personal equipment, which had been sent away with the rest of the army's baggage on the departure from Whitemarsh in mid-December. As late as January 11, he was trying to have it located—"among other things a Bed; end Irons, Plates, Dishes, and Kitchen utensils"—and sent to him at Valley

Forge.[92] To make matters worse, the steward whom Washington had hired the previous spring had to be dismissed.

This was Patrick Maguire, a recent arrival from Ireland. "I have the greatest reason to believe," Washington wrote on April 17, "that during the whole time of his employ, he took every opportunity of defrauding me. He is given to liquor, and where he dares take the liberty, very insolent." Bearing out Washington's observation is the fact that after being sent packing, Maguire brashly applied to the Pennsylvania authorities for appointment as a commissary, and apparently would have been given the position if Washington had not intervened.[93]

Washington's Negro servant, Billy Lee, saw to the general's personal comfort as best he could under the circumstances, and after Martha Washington arrived early in February, she undoubtedly relieved her husband of many of the household details which had distracted him earlier. It is likely that she was behind the celebration, such as it was, of his forty-fifth birthday on February 22. Following a necessarily austere dinner, he and his guests were treated to a serenade by the fifers and drummers of the 2d Continental Artillery, who had come to headquarters on their own initiative to honor the Commander-in-Chief. He himself did not go out to greet them, but Martha conveyed his thanks to the musicians and tipped them fifteen shillings.[94]

Washington may have been restrained by diffidence, but this event took place during the worst period of the army's famine, and less than a week after Washington had been writing of the danger of mutiny; only days before, a group of soldiers had respectfully but firmly told Nathanael Greene that it would be impossible to remain unless the supply situation was improved.[95] It seems possible that Washington suspected that what was ostensibly a musical compliment might in reality be a disguise for a deputation. If so, his action would provide an example, under the circumstances, of wise and tactful leadership.

And whatever his faults as a commander, Washington admired, respected, and—most important—understood his men. On December 17, just before moving to Valley Forge, he had issued a General Order saying that "The Commander in Chief with the highest satisfaction expresses his thanks to the officers and soldiers for the fortitude and patience with which they have sustained the fatigues of the Campaign." Conceding that there had been reverses, he insisted that "upon the whole Heaven hath smiled on our arms . . . and . . . by a spirited continuance of the measures necessary . . . we shall finally obtain . . . Independence, Liberty and Peace." After predicting open help from France, he told the army that "he persuades himself, that the officers and soldiers, with one heart, and one mind, will resolve to surmount every difficulty, with a fortitude and patience, be coming their profession, and the sacred cause in which they are engaged."[96]

Beginning with a commendation, moving on to an admission that hazards remained, then reassuring the troops with promises of improvement, and concluding with an expression of faith in the ability and determination which guarantee ultimate success, this order could serve as a model for inspirational messages. Again, following the horror of January and February, Washington issued a similar order on March 1, brightening it with a touch of wry humor. "Occasional distress for want of provisions and other necessities is a spectacle that frequently occurs in every army," he pointed out, then added that "perhaps there never was one which has been in general so plentifully supplied in respect to the former as ours."[97]

Soldiers are quick to see exhortation as hypocrisy, however, unless they are convinced of its sincerity. It is abundantly clear that Washington enjoyed the confidence and esteem of his men. Criticisms there were, but they came from the rest of the population, and they aroused indignation in the army. One diary stated on December 26,

> Why don't his Excellency rush in & retake the City [Phila-
> delphia] . . . ? Because he knows better than to leave his
> Post and be catch'd like a d----d fool cooped up in the City.
> He has always acted wisely hitherto. His conduct when closely
> scrutinised is uncensurable. Were his Inferior Generals as
> skillful as himself, we should have the grandest Choir of
> Officers ever God made. . . . His Excellency . . . is deserving
> of the greatest encomiums. . . . History will . . . reflect lasting
> honour on the Wisdom & prudence of G[enl] Washington.[98]

And Washington's standing did not deteriorate during the encampment. On March 20, another diarist wrote of the eventual recovery of Philadelphia that "We rely on the prudence and military skill of our worthy General, to accomplish this."[99]

Along with determination and patience, it was personality and force of character which were Washington's strong points, for notwithstanding the diarists' expressions of admiration and confidence, Washington's "military skill" was considered by many to be open to challenge. At Brandywine he had been deceived, and by the same ruse which Howe had used successfully at Long Island in 1776. He had been repeatedly outmaneuvered in his attempt to block British capture of Philadelphia. At Germantown, he had adopted a plan far too complicated for the state of his troops' training, and then had gone impulsively ahead with it in a piecemeal fashion. On grounds of short-range achievement, in fact, there was considerable basis for criticism.

And critics were not lacking in Congress, in the country at large, and in parts of the army not serving under Washington's direct command.

Indeed, the coalescence of criticism, seized upon by some who aspired to higher rank and greater influence in the army, resulted in the so-called "Conway Cabal," which was one of the most worrying distractions with which Washington had to deal during his winter at Valley Forge.

In brief, this was an intrigue aimed at replacing Washington as Commander-in-Chief with General Horatio Gates. From the standpoint of professional background, Gates's credentials were superior, as he had served for twenty years as a Regular officer in the British Army, experiencing considerable combat and reaching the rank of major. In terms of achievement during the Revolution, he had been credited with the victory at Saratoga in October, 1777; this was the most significant American success since the British were compelled to evacuate Boston, and in fact was to prove to be the military turning point of the entire war. While the army was at Valley Forge, Gates was at York as president of the Board of War which, under Congress, was roughly analogous to the modern Department of Defense. Gates himself was ambitious, and unquestionably considered himself superior to Washington as a soldier.

Lending the support of his influence and connections was General Thomas Mifflin, a prominent Pennsylvanian. He had served for a time as an aide to Washington, and then—although he wanted a field command—had been made Quartermaster General. In arguing with Washington about strategy (Mifflin wanted top priority given to holding Philadelphia), he came so close to insubordination that, on reflection, he became convinced that he had permanently antagonized Washington. Uninterested in his assignment as Quartermaster General, he gave it little attention, and although he resigned the post, Congress soon named him to the Board of War, in charge of supervising quartermaster activities.

The prime mover in the whole affair, however, was General Thomas Conway. Born in Ireland, he had grown up in France, served twenty-eight years in the French Army, and was a relatively senior colonel by the time he came to America in the spring of 1777. Appointed a brigadier general of Continentals, he had shown considerable ability, but his boastfulness and supercilious attitude toward American officers caused resentment in the army even while his adroit intriguing won him supporters in Congress. In the fall of 1777, Congress proposed his promotion to major general, but Washington objected that this would be unfair to a number of able and senior American brigadiers. Congress therefore withdrew the proposal, but when Conway threatened to resign unless he was promoted, Congress gave in and on December 14 named him not only to the higher rank but to the key post of Inspector General.

Conway had already begun to try to undermine Washington, presumably with the idea that his fortunes would be better served with Gates in command. As early as November 8, Washington had heard from Lord Stirling that Colonel James Wilkinson, Gates's aide, had told Stirling's aide, Major William McWilliams, that Conway had written to Gates that "Heaven has been determined to save your Country; or a weak General and bad Counsellors would have ruined it." Washington was less angered by the clear insult than by the implication that an officer under his immediate command was conspiring with another subordinate against him.[100] But he was anxious not to generate or publicize dissension, and he was preoccupied with tactical problems, so he limited himself merely to sending a note to Conway, written on November 9, which stated that he had been informed that Conway had allegedly made the statement to Gates.[101]

Nothing further developed until Conway reported at Valley Forge to take up his duties as Inspector General. Washington's reception of him was correct but frigid. Conway expressed his resentment in an impertinent letter, to which Washington replied dispassionately but coldly. Not content, Conway went a step further. In his next letter to Washington he compared Washington sarcastically (or so Washington interpreted it) to Frederick the Great, and went on to say that "by the complexion of your letter and by the reception you have honored me with since my arrival, I perceive that I have not the happiness of being agreeable to your Excellency and that I can expect no support in fulfilling the laborious duty of an Inspector General."[102]

Coldly furious at the suggestion that personal dislike would cause him to be derelict in his duty to a subordinate, on January 2 Washington sent copies of the whole exchange to the President of Congress, stating that "If General Conway means . . . that I did not receive him in the language of a warm and cordial Friend, I readily confess the charge. . . . My feelings will not permit me to make professions of friendship to the man I deem my enemy. . . ."[103]

Nor did Washington any longer consider Gates a friend. On December 31 he had written to Lafayette of Gates that

> His ambition and great desire of being puffed off as one of the first Officers of the Age, could only be equalled by the means which he used to obtain them; but finding that I was determined not to go beyond the line of my duty to indulge him in the first, nor, to exceed the strictest rules of propriety, to gratify him in the second, he became my inveterate Enemy; and has, I am persuaded, practised every Art to do me an injury. . . .[104]

Conway had by now told Gates that Washington had learned of their correspondence, and early in January Washington received a letter from Gates; this letter expressed concern because Gates's papers were being copied, but denied neither the relationship with Conway nor the accuracy of the alleged statement against Washington. Not only was this a strange reaction, but Gates also sent a copy of this letter to Congress. Washington felt compelled, therefore, to reply through the same channel, explaining in a letter of January 4 how he had been informed of Conway's offensive statement so as to eliminate any suggestion that he had been associated with any tampering with Gates's correspondence.[105]

Because there was opposition to Washington by some members of Congress, these criticisms were a potentially serious menace to him, and the problem was compounded by the rumors of dissatisfaction within the army which Mifflin tried to spread. To Washington's mind, a more significant danger than the threat to his own position was that factionalism might develop within the army. On the other hand, Washington also had strong Congressional support, which increased as the Committee on Conference reported the scale of the problems he faced. Further, Gates made the mistake of trying to dissemble, sending Washington a disclaimer which was incompatible with his earlier letter and in some respects even internally contradictory, but defending Conway and endorsing his military vision. In a long reply of January 23, Washington enumerated Gates's inconsistencies. Regarding Conway, he waxed sarcastic. "It is . . . greatly lamentable," he wrote, "that this adept in Military science did not employ his abilities in the progress of the Campaign, in pointing out those wise moves. . . . The United States have lost from that unseasonable diffidence, which prevented his . . . displaying those rich treasures of knowledge and experience he has since so freely laid open to you." Then, changing his tone, Washington asserted bitingly that "He is capable of all the malignity of detraction, and all the meanesses of intrigue, to gratify the absurd resentment of disappointed vanity, or to answer the purposes of personal aggrandizement, and promote the interests of faction."[106]

By this time, Gates apparently realized that he had overreached himself. As the Board of War was located at the temporary capital at York, he was in a good position to assess the attitude of Congress, many of whose members were beginning to reverse their originally favorable view of Conway. This, together with the steadfast support which such key officials as President Henry Laurens gave to Washington, led Gates on February 19 to write Washington a conciliatory letter; and on February 24, Washington replied, agreeing somewhat stiffly to drop the whole issue.[107] This essentially ended the matter, although some weeks later Benjamin Rush was still circulating a letter attacking Washington's competence.[108] But by February 28, Washington was convinced that the whole affair had blown over.[109] It was laid to rest permanently when, on April 22, Conway threatened to resign his commission and Congress promptly accepted.

In some respects, this episode might appear to be a tempest in a teapot. However, it had its serious aspects. For one thing, it demanded attention which Washington would have preferred to devote to the problems of the army, and added to burdens which were already staggering. For another, it held the potential of sowing disunion among men whose harmony and cooperation were vital if the war was to be won. In the end, though, Washington's standing had been reinforced, as the supporters of his principal rival had been firmly rejected by the bulk of Congress.

Through the period at Valley Forge, Washington's own morale ranged from near-hopelessness to genuine if somewhat qualified optimism. His forebodings during the first weeks of the encampment concerning the army's chances for mere survival have been noted, as well as the bleak view he took regarding the possibilities of mutiny and the implications of the many resignations. Since these views were expressed in efforts to wring support or cooperation, it may be that, for emphasis, Washington was painting the picture more darkly than he actually saw it. On the other hand, the rosiest view of the situation through February would necessarily have contained heavy overtones of black. As the winter passed, though, even before he had word of the French Alliance, Washington's mood changed. The General Orders of May 2 spoke of "the signal Instances of providential Goodness" which "have now almost crowned our labours with complete

Success...." This tone could have been adopted to hearten the troops, but on May 15, in a letter to a trusted Virginia friend, Washington wrote that "Matters appear abroad to be in as favourable a train as we could wish, and If we are not free and happy, it will be owing to a want of virtue, prudence, and management among ourselves."[110]

However close he may have come to despair, Washington was too able a leader to let his misgivings show to the men. The image he maintained of unruffled confidence undoubtedly generated, in its turn, confidence among the troops, despite the clear appearance of looming disaster. But as the situation bettered and Washington's own spirits rose, there were a few instances when even his iron self-control slipped briefly, letting the exuberance he was feeling show through. In particular, there was the day of the formal celebration of the French Alliance when, riding away from the final phase of the festivities to the cheers of his officers, he turned repeatedly, waving his hat in the air and shouting "Huzza!"[111]

In sum, the achievement of Valley Forge is in many respects due to Washington's personal influence. With all his technical limitations as a soldier, Washington possessed a quality which more than outweighed them. That was his capacity, matched by none of his potential rivals, for inspiring the esteem, affection, and trust of his followers. This quality was undeniably a key factor in the army's endurance of its long and agonizing ordeal.

VI

Highlights And Special Events

E VEN so bleak and dreary an experience as the Valley Forge encampment was not without its breaks in routine and occasions of particular interest.

After the low point of December 21, when there were insufficient provisions to put a force into the field against a British foraging party, the situation improved enough to permit a considerable amount of aggressive patrolling. Indeed, on December 22, a detachment and two cannon were sent out on a patrol that lasted a week.[1] Another force, of 150 men, was sent out on January 12,[2] but was back in camp within two days.[3] The same pace of activity apparently continued throughout the winter and spring.

Sometimes there were clashes with British detachments. The patrol which left on December 22 captured a dozen British dragoons, but lost eighteen men of its own.[4] Another engagement, particularly spectacular, took place on January 18. Captain Henry Lee, with Lieutenant William Lindsay and a force of Light Horse, had been ranging the area south of Valley Forge when he stopped for the night along the Sugartown road. The two officers and five of the cavalrymen found quarters in a farmhouse, and the rest of the unit in another house a considerable distance away. During the evening, Major John Jameson, 2d Continental Light Dragoons, dropped by to spend the night. Despite the mounted sentries Lee had posted, a force of upwards of two hundred British dragoons, commanded by Captain Banastre Tarleton and guided by local Tories, succeeded in surprising the house where Lee was quartered. There was barely time to bar the door, and the eight men in the house were not enough to cover all the windows. Nevertheless, by spirited fire and by moving quickly from window to window, they succeeded in driving off repeated assaults,[5] winning an official commendation in General Orders for "their superior Bravery and Address."[6]

Less dramatic, but of great importance in the long run, was the arrival at Valley Forge in late January of members of the Committee on Conference which Congress had appointed on January 10 to work with Washington in planning a consolidation of existing Continental battalions, selecting the officers whom the reorganization would displace, settling questions of rank, determining the number and sources of men to be recruited, and "in general, to adopt such other measures as they shall judge necessary for introducing oeconomy and promoting discipline and good morals [*sic*] in the army." The original members were Francis Dana, Joseph Reed, Nathaniel Folsom, and three members of the Board of War—Generals Gates and Mifflin and Colonel Timothy Pickering.[7] The latter three, pleading other duties, asked to be excused, and were replaced by Charles Carroll and Gouverneur Morris,[8] and on January 12, John Harvie was added to the committee.[9]

Meeting at Moore Hall (the house of William Moore, about two miles from Valley Forge), they held their first session on January 28,[10] and continued to sit frequently until well into April.[11] They made a conscientious effort to look searchingly into all the army's problems, to report their findings to Congress in detail, and to recommend solutions that were both positive and feasible. They played an important role in making Congress realize the straits into which the army had fallen; they helped make it possible for the able Nathanael Greene to be appointed Quartermaster General; and their persuasion was an important element in the adoption by Congress of reforms which, although sometimes falling short of what they and Washington advocated, made important contributions to the preservation of the army for the time being and the establishment of a sound basis for its continued operation in the future.

Just as the Committee on Conference meetings began, the troops at Valley Forge saw the departure for Albany, New York, of Generals Lafayette and De Kalb. The Board of War's first venture into strategy was to plan a raid—they called it an "irruption"—into Canada. Staffing the raiding force with French officers would incidentally provide employment for the numbers of French volunteers who could not be assigned to units without disrupting the seniority lists, and would also (it was hoped) encourage collaboration by French Canadians against the British. Washington had little confidence in the plan, which, he wrote on February 8, "I am well persuaded is the child of folly, and must be productive of capital ills . . . ; but as it is the first fruit of our new board of War, I did not incline to say any thing against it."[12]

He was a sound prophet. Too few troops were available; there were quarrels over command arrangements; bad weather imposed delays and prevented use of the more direct route that had been planned. On March 13, Congress ordered the operation abandoned, and a week later Washington was sending orders for Lafayette and De Kalb to return to Valley Forge.[13]

At the camp, meanwhile, legend has it that an episode occurred which could be viewed either as evidence of high spirits or an incipient riot with overtones of regional resentments.

Supposedly, it began early on March 17, when some soldiers of one of the Pennsylvania regiments made a sort of scarecrow, labeled it "Paddy," and set it up beside the sector of Colonel Daniel Morgan's 11th Virginia, many of whose members were Irishmen or of Irish extraction. Discovering it, they took deep offense, but made the mistake of blaming Massachusetts troops for this insult. Morgan's men were as hard-bitten as any in the army; the New Englanders disliked Virginians in any case, and were full of outraged innocence. Apparently there was a considerable exchange of noisy threats, but Washington—summoned by an apprehensive Officer of the Day—arrived on the scene before there had been any actual violence.

The story has it that a quick check convinced Washington that no one really knew who had set up the offending scarecrow. Showing a clear grasp of soldier psychology, he put on a fine display of fury, outdoing even the Virginians in his anger. He was a great admirer of St. Patrick, he announced, and he would not tolerate such an outrage. All he wanted was to be told who in fact was responsible, and he would see to it that the culprit was made permanently regretful. Confronted with more support than they had bargained for, and unable to identify who had actually set up the "Paddy," Morgan's men began to feel rather sheepish—as Washington must have anticipated. To save face all around, he gave orders for a gill of spirits to be issued to each soldier, turning a potentially nasty situation into an impromptu celebration.[14]

No contemporary record, official or otherwise, has been found to substantiate this story. Further, considering the high percentage of Irish-born soldiers in the Pennsylvania regiments, it seems doubtful that they would have played such a prank. On the other hand, the solution attributed to Washington has the ring of practical leadership technique, and while the story may be as apocryphal as the one about the fabled cherry tree, it makes a valid point regarding Washington's ability as a troop commander.

Whatever the truth of the St. Patrick's Day story, April brought several special events. Major General Charles Lee, who had been a prisoner of war since 1776, was finally paroled as a preliminary to his imminent exchange. On April 6, he was welcomed to camp with great ceremony. A member of Washington's Life Guard, misdating the event in his diary as April 5, wrote that "Gen. Washington with all his attendence went to the [outpost] Lines to Meet Gen. Lee and to

Accompany him to the Head Quarters where they arrived at two of the Clock in the afternoon where they was receved with a kind salute of arms Drums fifes and Band of Musick."[15] That evening, Lee was the Washingtons' guest of honor at what Elias Boudinot described as "an Elegant Dinner, and the Music Playing the whole time," and for the night was given a bedroom directly behind Martha Washington's sitting room. Boudinot, who made no secret of his loathing for Lee, continued the account somewhat waspishly:

> The next morning he lay very late, and Breakfast was delayed for him. When he came out, he looked as dirty as if he had been in the Street all night. Soon after I discovered that he had brought a miserable dirty hussy with him from Philadelphia (a British Sergeants wife) and had actually taken her into his Room by a Back Door and she had slept with him that night.[16]

Lee's return would have been of direct interest chiefly to the more senior officers, and any scandal concerning him would have been kept as quiet as possible. May 1, however, saw an event which involved the bulk of the soldiers.

The day had been adopted as its special holiday by a super-patriots' organization called the Society of King Tammany, taking its name from a friendly Indian leader who had lived in Pennsylvania some decades earlier. The celebration of the day at Valley Forge was planned and carried out exclusively by the enlisted men, and from the accounts of observers, preparations must have been extensive.

At reveille, "mirth and Jollity" began which lasted all day. Soldiers, wearing white blossoms in their hats, followed their fifers and drummers in parading past the May poles which had been erected in every regimental area. The 3d New Jersey, whose ceremony may have been exceptionally elaborate, had one sergeant in Indian costume representing "King" Tammany leading the procession; behind him, in line abreast, came thirteen sergeants, dressed in white, each carrying a bow in his left hand and thirteen arrows in his right; then came thirteen drummers and fifers; and finally, thirteen platoons of thirteen men each. After giving three cheers at their May pole, they trooped off to Washington's headquarters to cheer the Commander-in-Chief. "But just as they were descending the hill to the house an Aide [Captain John Marshall, later Chief Justice of the Supreme Court] met them and informed them that the General was indisposed and desird them to retire. . . ." Despite the fact that the description makes the whole episode sound orderly and well controlled, there must have been a real fear that what was probably a somewhat rowdy celebration might get out of bounds. In any case, the officer who described the affair showed obvious relief in reporting that the men left the headquarters area "with the greatest decency and regularity." Marching back to their own sector, they cheered at each May pole they passed. Then, after "taking a drink of Whiskey which a Generous contribution of their officers had procured for them they dismisd and each man retird to his own hut without any incident hapening throughout the whole day the whole being carried on with the greatest regularity." The officers, somewhat more sedate, gathered in the evening and "had a song and dance in honour of King Tamany" which lasted until midnight.[17]

A still greater celebration—undoubtedly the highlight of the entire encampment—took place on May 6. This was the formal observance of the Treaty of Alliance between France and the United States, in a day set aside for "rejoysing throughout the whole Army."[18]

Detailed instructions were issued in General Orders.[19] Brigades assembled at 9 A.M. for an hour and a half of prayer and "discourse" by their chaplains. At 10:30, on a signal fired from the artillery park, the men fell in for inspection. An hour later, following another cannon shot, the brigades wheeled by platoons to march to their parade positions, forming two long ranks. Meanwhile, "Thirteen six Pounders were drove to a height in the rear of Conways Brigade."[20] Then Washington reviewed the formation, riding from the right to the left of the front line, then back along the second rank, after which he, his aides, and the Life Guard took post on a slight rise to the right rear.[21] At this juncture, the flag on Fort Washington was lowered and a third gun was fired from the artillery park. This was the signal for the field pieces on the hill to begin a thirteen-gun salute. As soon as this was completed, a *feu de joie* of musketry rippled down the front rank from right to left, then down the second rank from left to right. The order went on to specify that "The whole Army will Huzza! 'Long Live the King of France.'" Then came another thirteen-gun salute from the heights, another *feu de joie*, and a cheer, "Long Live the Friendly European Powers." The same procedure was carried out a third time, ending with a cheer, "To the American States." The order concluded with the directive that "Each man is to have a Gill of rum."

Actually, not quite the whole army could be on hand to enjoy the celebration. Morgan's Virginians were sent to patrol the area between Valley Forge and Philadelphia. "The reason for this," their orders stated, "is that the enemy may think to take advantage of the cele-

bration of this day. The troops must have more than the common
quantity of liquor, and perhaps there will be some little drunkenness
among them."[22]

Despite the intricacy of the ceremony, one of the officers present
claimed that "The order with which the whole was conducted, the
beautiful effect of the running fire, which was executed to perfection,
the martial appearance of the troops, gave sensible pleasure to every
one present. . . . The plan, as formed by Baron de Steuben, succeeded
in every particular," and he concluded perceptively that this "is in
a great measure attributed to his unwearied attention. . . ."[23]

But this was not the end. "There was a grand harber [arbor] bilt,"
a member of the Life Guard noted, "and all the Commissioners [com-
missioned officers] were Envited to dine with His Exelency."[24] There
they enjoyed a "cold collation . . . where many patriotic Toasts were
drank and the [day] concluded with harmless Mirth and jollity."[25]
In the course of the meal, "Triumph beamed in every countenance.
. . . The General received such proofs of the love and attachment of
his officers as must have given him the most exquisite feelings."[26]
Given the warmth of emotion, the significance of the occasion, and
perhaps the number of toasts, it is hardly surprising that as Washington rode away he split the air with repeated shouts of "Huzza!"

Problems continued, however. Only a week before, a detachment
of about two hundred Pennsylvania militia under Brigadier General
John Lacey, stationed in Bucks County to interfere with British traffic
north from Philadelphia, had been surprised asleep in the vicinity of
the Crooked Billet Tavern. Lacey and some of his men escaped, only
to find their route blocked by British cavalry. Ordering a charge, the
militia brigadier and his men cut their way through and eventually
reached safety. But eight to ten of the Pennsylvanians had been
wounded in the original surprise, a number were missing, and twenty-
six were killed—several of these had been cut down after being
wounded, and some had been burned to death when the British set
fire to piles of straw where they were hiding. The officer in charge
of the sentries, who had found shelter when the rainy night had grown
chilly and thus had allowed the British to approach undetected, was
dismissed.[27] Lacey was exonerated by an enquiry, but Washington—
in contrast to his reaction to Henry Lee's experience in January—
wrote stiffly to him that "You may depend that this will ever be the
consequence of permitting yourself to be surprised."[28]

Another problem now coming to a head concerned the oaths of
allegiance and abjuration which, by a Congressional directive of Feb-

ruary 3, all officers were required to take.[29] Looking to the temper of his officers at the time, Washington had deliberately procrastinated, but by early May the situation had eased sufficiently for him to decide that he could now carry out his instructions. Accordingly, a General Order of May 7 announced the requirement and established a procedure to be followed "in order to carry out this very interesting and essential work as soon as possible."[30]

As Washington had anticipated, however, there were difficulties. There was a shortage of blank forms for the oath, and an adequate supply was still not available as late as May 28. In addition, there were reservations on the part of many officers. On May 11, Washington was urging Lord Stirling to administer the oaths as soon as possible to the officers of the 3d and 4th New Jersey regiments, who had overcome their objections, "as there is some little boggle in this matter in other Corps . . . [and] it will be a good example to others." Apparently, the example worked for all units except one. That was Woodford's Virginia brigade. Some twenty-six of its officers protested the requirement on grounds that it implied an indignity; that it would freeze their existing ranks (about which there were some unsettled arguments) ; that it would preclude either their promotions or their resignations; and that it committed them to acceptance of the existing establishment, thus making any of the needed changes for improvement impossible of adoption. Patiently, Washington replied to the complaint, refuting the objections item by item.[31] This satisfied the officers and they were duly sworn.

At this same time, the most ambitious of the forays from Valley Forge against the British was taking place. Numerous rumors had reached the camp that the British were preparing to evacuate Philadelphia. Washington decided to send a detachment closer to the city to learn what could be verified. If the rumors were true and an evacuation was imminent, such a detachment should be large enough to pursue and harass the British rear. Consequently, he formed a task force of over two thousand troops, including part of his Life Guard and the recently arrived Oneida Indians, giving command to Lafayette.

Crossing the Schuylkill at Swede's Ford soon after midnight on May 19, the Americans marched toward Germantown, halting about twelve miles from Philadelphia at Barren Hill and deploying to its southeast in a line running in an arc southwestward from the Germantown Pike on the east to high ground overlooking the river, on the southern face of the hill. Pennsylvania militia cavalry was supposed to be taking position along the road leading toward Whitemarsh in case any British party should approach, and combination Indian and Continental Light Dragoon patrols were covering the approaches to the front.

After dawn, Lafayette began seeking some local residents who would be willing to go into Philadelphia to report on what the British were doing. But the British were already aware of the American move, and had plans afoot for a massive attack by multiple columns to encircle and capture the force at Barren Hill. Howe himself would lead one column, following a road that led to the front of the American position. General Charles Grey was to lead a second column, with the objective of hitting the American left flank. The third column, under General James Grant, would make a wide swing to the north, well beyond Barren Hill, then cut southeast to get between Barren Hill and the nearest ford to its rear.

While these plans were being laid, the troops waited and amused themselves as best they could. Some of the Indians were showing the soldiers how accurate they were with their bows when a soldier asked one of them to shoot at a strange mass in a corner of the roof of an abandoned building on the hill's top. The Oneida obligingly let fly an arrow and disturbed a huge cluster of bats.

> The house was immediately alive with them, and it was like-wise instantly full of Indians and soldiers. The poor bats fared hard. . . . They killed I know not how many. . . . I never saw so many bats before nor since.[32]

After dark on May 19, the British began to move, Grant in the lead. The Pennsylvania militia supposedly covering the road on which he marched had never taken position, and Grant was beyond Whitemarsh when a militia captain happened to see the column and hurried to Barren Hill with the news.[33] As for the scouts to the front, the Oneidas proved to be a disappointment. One soldier observed that "The Indians, with all their alertness, had like to have 'bought the rabbit.' "[34] The Light Dragoons had done better, for soon after the original alert, a courier arrived from their commander, stating that the outposts had captured two British soldiers who had reported that a major attack force was on the way. The word that spread among the troops at Barren Hill was that "the howl [whole] of Gen. How's Army was Advansing upon us in three Colloms. . . . The Nuse alarmed [alerted] us Enstantly. . . ."[35]

The only solution was to race Grant's column to Matson's Ford. To increase his chances, Lafayette sent a detachment with two field pieces to try to delay the British advance. Fortunately, on glimpsing the American rear guard through a screen of timber, Grant mistook its rear for its front; driving in to strike what he believed to be the column's center, he found his intended prey well out of range.[36] The escape was not completed without further difficulty, however. One of the Life Guardsmen bringing up the rear reported that, crossing the Schuylkill,

> . . . the warter was up to our middle and run very swift so that we were obliged to hold to each other to keep the Corrent from sweeping us away and all in a fluster expecting the Enemy to fire in upon us for we could see them Plain but the reason was they Could not git thare Cannon to bare on us but we got all Safe across without the loss of any save fore or five of our party that the Enemy's Lite horse Cut to pieces and our flanks killed three of there Lite Draghoons and four of there Granadears.[37]

Lafayette deployed his force to cover the southern end of the ford, but the British were unwilling to attack across the river and, about 2 P.M., started back to Philadelphia. The Americans bivouacked at Gulph Mills. Next morning, Lafayette moved upstream to Swede's Ford, crossed the river, and returned to Barren Hill, remaining there until May 23, when the whole force marched back to Valley Forge.

Tactically, this operation accomplished very little. It did have value, however, in demonstrating to the army as a whole the progress that had been made in training and discipline. Washington reported to Congress that, although attacked without warning, the force had performed efficiently and had "made a timely and handsome retreat in great order over the Schuylkill. . . ."[38]

From that time on, all energies at Valley Forge were directed toward preparations for resuming an active campaign in pursuit of the British as soon as Philadelphia was abandoned. The work was carried out to good effect, for when word reached Valley Forge just before noon on June 18 that the British had left the city during the night, the Americans were ready to start one division moving in pursuit before the afternoon was over. The rest of the army followed on June 19, six months to the day after they had come limping in to begin their winter encampment.

William Alexander (Lord Stirling),
by Bass Otis after Sir Joshua Reynolds

VII

Epilogue

O<small>N</small> June 28, little more than a week after leaving Valley Forge, the leading American elements caught up with the withdrawing British. The Battle of Monmouth, which then took place, was inconclusive. The failure of the Americans to win a clear-cut victory was not due, however, to any ineptitude on the part of the troops. Rather, it resulted from misjudgment of the situation and consequent mishandling of forces by the senior commander on the spot, General Charles Lee. It seems clear that one of the chief factors influencing Lee that day was the same lack of confidence in the American soldier which he had freely expressed (with considerable reason at the time) prior to his capture in the fall of 1776. Probably it is significant that, not having been released by the British until April, 1778, Lee had had little opportunity to observe and appreciate the changes which had been wrought by the Valley Forge experience.

Monmouth, it is true, was the last major Revolutionary War engagement fought in the north. Until the siege of Yorktown in the autumn of 1781—where over half the force was provided by Rochambeau's French regiments—the troops under Washington's immediate command saw no further combat much larger than patrol actions, except for an occasional limited-objective raid such as Anthony Wayne's attack on Stony Point, New York, in July, 1779. Thus, there are no spectacular operations which can be pointed out as offering neatly conclusive demonstrations of the military mutation which the army had undergone. Nevertheless, it still can be stated confidently that the winter of 1777-1778 saw the development of the Continental forces into what was for the first time a genuine army.

Although Washington's army as a whole experienced no more pitched battles for the next three years, some of its units were detached to serve in the south under Gates and later under Nathanael Greene. They were defeated more often than they were victorious, but the effect of their training can be seen, if nowhere else, in the mere fact that despite repeated near-disasters, they held together. Other units took part in John Sullivan's 1779 expedition deep into the Iroquois country of New York State. They saw little fighting, but such combat as they had was admirably carried out and during the whole campaign they demonstrated thorough professionalism in the face of great difficulties and hazards.

The most significant point is that, at Valley Forge, doctrinal differences had been ironed out, a single body of regulations had been adopted, willing but ignorant officers as well as men had been schooled in their duties, and a level of standards of performance had been established. Thus, not only directly through the performance of the veterans of Valley Forge but (even more importantly) *indirectly*, by the spread throughout the service of the values these men had learned, the Valley Forge experience must be recognized as one of the major turning points of the war, ranking with the decision to declare independence, the attack on Trenton, Burgoyne's surrender at Saratoga, and Cornwallis' defeat at Yorktown.

At Valley Forge itself, on June 19, 1778, there can have been few regrets among the soldiers who stepped out smartly, leaving the camp behind them. But regardless of the misery of the preceding months, they and the nation just coming into being had gained something of lasting value.

These soldiers were a far cry from the ragged, freezing, half-starved collection of men who had begun the encampment. They had become an army—proficient in the skills of their trade, cohesive and responsive to their leaders, and for the first time competently and responsibly led. The road that lay ahead was long and full of adversities, but since December the army had taken a giant step toward achievement of the new nation's ultimate goal of firmly established independence.

Thus, the country as a whole had gained a major benefit in terms of its immediate objective. And, for the first time, an instrument had been forged which would provide one of the major safeguards of that nation throughout the years to come.

Notes

I. THE ROAD TO MOUNT JOY

1. Frank H. Taylor, *Valley Forge: A Chronicle of American Heroism* (Philadelphia: James W. Nagle, Publisher, 1905), p. 13.
2. Howard M. Jenkins, "The Old Iron Forge—'Valley Forge,'" *Pennsylvania Magazine of History and Biography*, XVII (1893), 432-33.
3. *Ibid.*, pp. 433-35, 441.
4. Arthur Cecil Bining, *Pennsylvania Iron Manufacture in the Eighteenth Century* (Harrisburg: Pennsylvania Historical Commission, 1938), p. 30.
5. *Ibid.*, p. 115.
6. Jenkins, pp. 438, 441-42.
7. John F. Reed, *Valley Forge, Crucible of Victory* (Monmouth Beach, New Jersey: Philip Freneau Press, 1969), p. 58. (Cited hereafter as Reed, *Valley Forge.*)
8. Harry Emerson Wildes, *Valley Forge* (New York: The Macmillan Company, 1938), pp. 8-9.
9. *Captain* John Montrésor, "Journal, July 1, 1777 to July 1, 1778," *Pennsylvania Magazine of History and Biography*, VI (1882), 39, 41.
10. Jenkins, p. 430.
11. Douglas Southall Freeman, *George Washington* (New York: Charles Scribner's Sons, 1951), IV, 427.
12. Donald Barr Chidsey, *Valley Forge* (New York: Crown Publishers, Inc., 1956, 1966), p. 10.
13. Montrésor, p. 38.
14. *The Journals of Henry Melchior Muhlenberg* (Philadelphia: The Muhlenberg Press, 1958), III, 78.
15. John F. Reed, *Campaign to Valley Forge* (Philadelphia: University of Pennsylvania Press, 1965), p. 176.
16. Montrésor, p. 39.
17. George Weedon, *Valley Forge Orderly Book* (New York: Dodd, Mead and Company, 1902), p. 95.
18. Ray Thompson, *Washington at Whitemarsh: Prelude to Valley Forge* (Fort Washington, Pa.: The Bicentennial Press, n. d.), pp. 7-8, 14.
19. Reed, *Campaign*, p. 365.
20. Weedon, p. 138.
21. Reed, *Campaign*, p. 366.
22. Joseph Plumb Martin, *Private Yankee Doodle* (Boston: Little, Brown and Company, 1962), p. 98.
23. *Elijah Fisher's Journal* (Augusta, Me.: Press of Badger and Manley, 1880), p. 7.
24. Quoted, Wildes, pp. 140-41.
25. *Dr.* Albigence Waldo, "Valley Forge, 1777-1778. Diary of Surgeon Albigence Waldo, of the Connecticut Line," *Pennsylvania Magazine of History and Biography*, XXI (1897), 308.
26. Martin, p. 100.
27. Reed, *Valley Forge*, p. 5.

II. "UNLESS SOME GREAT AND CAPITAL CHANGE TAKES PLACE . . ."

1. Taylor, p. 22.
2. Reed, *Valley Forge*, p. 5.
3. Martin, p. 103.

4. John C. Fitzpatrick (ed.), *The Writings of George Washington From the Original Manuscript Sources, 1744-1799* (Washington: United States Government Printing Office, 1933), X, 192.

5. Weedon, pp. 160-61.

6. William A. Ganoe, *The History of the United States Army* (New York: D. Appleton-Century Company, Inc., 1942), p. 52.

7. Thomas Paine, "Military Operations Near Philadelphia in the Campaign of 1777-1778. Described in a Letter from Thomas Paine to Dr. Franklin," *Pennsylvania Magazine of History and Biography,* II (1878), 294.

8. Reed, *Valley Forge,* p. 13.

9. Weedon, pp. 163-64.

10. Chidsey, p. 138.

11. Reed, *Valley Forge,* p. 12.

12. Wildes, p. 152.

13. Waldo, p. 317.

14. Fitzpatrick, X, 170-71.

15. *Ibid.,* X, 170.

16. Joseph Clark, "Diary," *Proceedings of the New Jersey Historical Society,* VII (1855), 103.

17. Weedon, p. 161.

18. Fitzpatrick, X, 272-73.

19. Charles Knowles Bolton, *The Private Soldier Under Washington* (New York: Charles Scribner's Sons, 1902), p. 76.

20. Freeman, IV, 566 note 9.

21. George Washington Greene, *The Life of Nathanael Greene* (New York: Hurd and Houghton, 1871), II, 45.

22. Fitzpatrick, X, 170.

23. Chidsey, p. 22.

24. Reed, *Valley Forge,* pp. 16, 23.

25. Fitzpatrick, X, 432.

26. Bolton, p. 76.

27. Fitzpatrick, XI, 387.

28. Waldo, p. 321.

29. Weedon, pp. 184-85.

30. Fitzpatrick, XI, 463.

31. Greene, II, 44.

32. Weedon, p. 165.

33. Reed, *Valley Forge,* p. 18.

34. Quoted in Louis Gottschalk, *Lafayette Joins the American Army* (Chicago: The University of Chicago Press, 1937), p. 104.

35. Chidsey, p. 26.

36. Martin, pp. 103-104.

37. Reed, *Valley Forge,* p. 18.

38. Fitzpatrick, X, 268, 300, 320, 347.

39. Reed, *Valley Forge,* p. 29.

40. Greene, II, 46.

41. Fitzpatrick, X, 442, 464, 483.

42. Noah Brooks, *Henry Knox* (New York: G. P. Putnam's Sons, 1900), pp. 114-15.

43. Weedon, pp. 178-79.

44. Fitzpatrick, XI, 85.

45. *Ibid.,* XI, 135.

46. *Ibid.,* XI, 205, 279.

47. Greene, I, 541.

48. Chidsey, p. 26.

49. Weedon, p. 180.

50. *Ibid.*, p. 239.

51. *Ibid.*, p. 217.

52. Fitzpatrick, X, 412.

53. Greene, I, 541-42.

54. Fitzpatrick, X, 285, 341.

55. George Ewing, *The Military Journal of George Ewing, A Soldier of Valley Forge* (New York, 1928).

56. Weedon, pp. 209-10, 266, 273, 290.

57. *Ibid.*, p. 264.

58. Fitzpatrick, X, 199.

59. Weedon, pp. 182, 188, 190.

60. *Ibid.*, p. 209.

61. *Ibid.*, pp. 195-96.

62. Greene, II, 45-46.

63. Brooks, p. 115.

64. Fitzpatrick, X, 432, 464.

65. *Ibid.*, XI, 322, 394, 446.

66. Chidsey, p. 102.

67. Fitzpatrick, X, 194-95, 209, 224.

68. Weedon, pp. 169-70.

69. *Ibid.*, pp. 173-74, 196.

70. *Ibid.*, pp. 176, 179.

71. Fitzpatrick, X, 267.

72. Waldo, p. 322.

73. Reed, *Valley Forge*, p. 26.

74. Fitzpatrick, X, 218, 223.

75. William Chauncey Ford (ed.), *Journals of the Continental Congress* (Washington: Government Printing Office, 1908), X, 23.

76. Weedon, p. 192.

77. Fitzpatrick, X, 345.

78. Weedon, p. 208.

79. *Ibid.*, pp. 202-203, 207.

80. Fitzpatrick, X, 358.

81. Ford, X, 84.

82. Reed, *Valley Forge*, pp. 18, 45.

83. Ganoe, p. 52.

84. Fitzpatrick, X, 386.

85. *Ibid.*, X, 448, 482.

86. Quoted in Taylor, p. 46.

87. John Laurens, *The Army Correspondence of Colonel John Laurens in the Years 1777-8* (New York: Arno Press, Inc., 1969), p. 131.

88. Weedon, pp. 240-42.

89. Fitzpatrick, X, 517.

90. Quoted in Joseph B. Doyle, *Frederick William von Steuben and the American Revolution* (New York: Burt Franklin, 1913, 1970), p. 84.

91. John McAuley Palmer, *General von Steuben* (New Haven: Yale University Press, 1937), p. 137.

92. Fitzpatrick, XI, 35, 37.

93. Weedon, pp. 251-52.

94. Reed, *Valley Forge*, pp. 43, 46.

95. Weedon, p. 278.

96. Fitzpatrick, XI, 205, 220, 228-29.

97. Ford, X, 312.

98. Fitzpatrick, XI, 318, 429, 462.

99. Reed, Valley Forge, p. 27.

100. Weedon, pp. 200, 205, 228-29.

101. John Joseph Stoudt, *Ordeal at Valley Forge* (Philadelphia: University of Pennsylvania Press, 1963), pp. 127, 235.

102. Harry Emerson Wildes, *Anthony Wayne* (New York: Harcourt, Brace and Company, 1941), pp. 153-56. (Cited hereafter as Wildes, *Wayne*.)

103. Weedon, pp. 190, 219.

104. Elizabeth F. Ellet, *Women of the American Revolution* (Philadelphia: George W. Jacobs & Co., 1900), II, 273.

105. Martin, p. 111.

106. Waldo, p. 310.

107. Fitzpatrick, X, 327.

108. Reed, *Valley Forge*, p. 45.

109. Chidsey, p. 31.

110. Fitzpatrick, X, 401.

111. Greene, II, 46.

112. Quoted, *ibid.*, II, 44.

113. Chidsey, p. 119.

114. Reed, *Valley Forge*, p. 18.

115. Wildes, *Wayne*, pp. 147-48.

III. "THE POOR SICK, SUFFER MUCH . . . THIS COLD WEATHER"

1. Taylor, p. 14.

2. Louis C. Duncan, *Medical Men in the American Revolution 1775-1783* (Carlisle Barracks, Pa.: Medical Field Service School, 1931), p. 212.

3. Ford, XI, 539-41.

4. Waldo, p. 312.

5. Weedon, pp. 169, 175.

6. Quoted in Greene, II, 44-45.

7. Fitzpatrick, XI, 451, 469.

8. *Ibid.*, XI, 487-88; XII, 50, 76.

9. Fisher, p. 7.

10. Duncan, p. 221.

11. Reed, *Valley Forge*, p. 25.

12. Fitzpatrick, X, 233.

13. Duncan, pp. 221-22.

14. *Ibid.*, p. 223.

15. Fisher, p. 7.

16. Reed, *Valley Forge*, p. 48.

17. Duncan, p. 225.

18. Weedon, pp. 188, 191.

19. *Ibid.*, p. 204

20. *Ibid.*, pp. 192-93.

21. Greene, II, 44.

22. Weedon, p. 239.

23. *Ibid.*, pp. 193. 216, 243, 291, 299.

24. Duncan, p. 222.

25. Weedon, pp. 181, 186, 190.

26. *Ibid.*, pp. 185, 242-43, 251, 254-55.

27. *Ibid.*, pp. 285, 288-89, 305-306.

28. Laurens, p. 182.

29. Fitzpatrick, XI, 387.

30. Weedon, p. 183.
31. Waldo, pp. 321-22.
32. Greene, II, 45.
33. Weedon, pp. 263-64.
34. Fisher, p. 7.
35. Hugh F. Rankin, *The American Revolution* (New York: G. P. Putnam's Sons, 1964), p. 176.
36. Quoted in Taylor, p. 46.
37. Reed, *Valley Forge*, p. 28.
38. Waldo, pp. 316, 321.
39. Chidsey, p. 70.
40. Duncan, pp. 214, 224, 226.
41. Fitzpatrick, XI, 492.

IV. "IT WAS A CONTINUAL DRILL"

1. Weedon, pp. 160, 192.
2. Reed, *Valley Forge*, pp. 19-20; Alfred Hoyt Bill, *Valley Forge* (New York: Harper & Brothers, 1952), p. 95.
3. Weedon, pp. 201-202, 211, 272-73.
4. *Ibid.*, pp. 278-79.
5. Reed, *Valley Forge*, p. 21.
6. Freeman, IV, 627.
7. Weedon, pp. 84, 96.
8. Ganoe, p. 4.
9. Doyle, pp. 82-83.
10. Stoudt, p. 35.
11. *Ibid.*, p. 52.
12. Fitzpatrick, X, 210.
13. *Ibid.*, XII, 76.
14. *Ibid.*, X, 373.
15. *Ibid.*, XII, 30-32.
16. Ganoe, p. 10.
17. Doyle, p. 84.
18. *Ibid.*, p. 84.
19. Weedon, pp. 164-65.
20. Fitzpatrick, X, 314; XI, 133.
21. *Ibid.*, X, 181.
22. Stoudt, pp. 55, 225.
23. Fitzpatrick, XI, 322, 416, 422, 459; XII, 25.
24. *Ibid.*, X, 231, 431.
25. Weedon, p. 188.
26. Fitzpatrick, X, 277-78, 530; XI, 34.
27. *Ibid.*, X, 216, 248; XI, 156.
28. *Ibid.*, XI, 408; XII, 1.
29. Doyle, p. 84.
30. Palmer, p. 142.
31. Quoted in Doyle, p. 84.
32. Chidsey, p. 111.
33. Palmer, pp. 9, 18, 63.
34. *Ibid.*, pp. 27, 33-50.
35. Laurens, p. 137.
36. Palmer, pp. 49-55, 64, 80, 91, 94.
37. *Ibid.*, pp. 95-96.

38. *Ibid.*, pp. 123-24, 129-30, 136.
39. *Ibid.*, pp. 131-33.
40. *Ibid.*, pp. 100, 136, 138, 140.
41. *Ibid.*, p. 141.
42. *Ibid.*, p. 142.
43. Taylor, p. 82.
44. Weedon, p. 263.
45. Ganoe, p. 55.
46. Chidsey, p. 115.
47. Palmer, p. 148.
48. Chidsey, p. 122.
49. Ganoe, pp. 11, 56, 57.
50. Weedon, p. 266.
51. Palmer, pp. 147, 151.
52. *Ibid.*, p. 167.
53. Taylor, p. 83.
54. Weedon, pp. 285-86.
55. Martin, p. 118.
56. Palmer, pp. 152-53.
57. Ganoe, pp. 58-60.
58. Palmer, pp. 158, 165-66.
59. Weedon, p. 168.
60. *Ibid.*, pp. 183, 201, 248, 297-98, 300-301.
61. Fitzpatrick, XI, 156.
62. *Ibid.*, XII, 8.
63. *Ibid.*, X, 347-48.
64. *Ibid.*, X, 276.
65. *Ibid.*, X, 332.
66. Stoudt, pp. 115, 120-21.
67. Fitzpatrick, X, 427, 470 note 22, 476; XI, 181, 417.
68. Chidsey, p. 26.
69. Ford, V, 670 note 2, 788.
70. Fitzpatrick, X, 376, 402-403.
71. *Ibid.*, X, 115.
72. *Ibid.*, X, 273.
73. Weedon, pp. 186, 188.
74. Fitzpatrick, X, 320.
75. *Ibid.*, XI, 11-12.
76. *Ibid.*, X, 404; XI, 253, 265.
77. *Ibid.*, XI, 353-54.
78. *Ibid.*, XI, 356, 362
79. See Harry S. Blaine, *Who Stole the Shoes at Valley Forge? A Tragedy and Vindication* (Toledo, Ohio, 1966).
80. Reed, *Valley Forge*, p. 65.
81. Fitzpatrick, XII, 14.
82. *Ibid.*, X, 265-66.
83. *Ibid.*, XI, 83-84.
84. *Lieutenant* James McMichael, "Diary, 1776-1778," *Pennsylvania Archives, Second Series*, XV, 217.
85. Fitzpatrick, X, 434.
86. *Ibid.*, X, 312, 351.
87. McMichael, p. 217.
88. Fitzpatrick, XII, 7-8.
89. *Ibid.*, X, 258; XI, 19-20.

90. *Ibid.*, X, 342.
91. *Ibid.*, XI, 133, 254, 426.
92. Weedon, pp. 187, 214-16.
93. Fitzpatrick, X, 360.
94. *Ibid.*, XI, 143, 266, 487; XII, 49-50.
95. *Ibid.*, X, 360; XI, 265, 274, 489.
96. Weedon, p. 310
97. Fitzpatrick, XI, 156.
98. *Ibid.*, X, 500
99. *Ibid.*, X, 434, 436; XI, 11, 142-43, 254, 317.

V. THE PEOPLE

1. Wildes, p. 188.
2. Waldo, pp. 319-20.
3. Fitzpatrick, X, 400.
4. Ford, X, 221.
5. Fitzpatrick, XI, 390.
6. Martin, p. 118.
7. Fitzpatrick, XII, 56.
8. Quoted in Bolton, p. 22.
9. Benjamin Quarles, *The Negro in the American Revolution* (Chapel Hill: University of North Carolina Press, 1961), p. 11.
10. Reed, *Valley Forge*, p. 45.
11. Fitzpatrick, X, 400 note 36.
12. Laurens, pp. 108-109, 114-18.
13. Ganoe, p. 56.
14. Fitzpatrick, XI, 98-99.
15. Quoted in Duncan, p. 241.
16. *Ibid.*, p. 241.
17. Chidsey, p. 98.
18. Fitzpatrick, XII, 30-32.
19. *Ibid.*, X, 259, 284, 287-88, 462; XI, 56.
20. *Ibid.*, X, 418, 442, 462, 502; XII, 22-23.
21. *Ibid.*, X, 396
22. *Ibid.*, X, 193, 461, 469.
23. Quoted in Doyle, p. 86.
24. Fitzpatrick, XI, 117.
25. *Ibid.*, XI, 345.
26. *Ibid.*, X, 433-34; XI, 162, 346, 366.
27. *Ibid.*, X, 242.
28. Bolton, p. 162.
29. Chidsey, pp. 79-80.
30. Fitzpatrick, XI, 252, 342-43.
31. Chidsey, p. 130.
32. Ewing.
33. Fitzpatrick, X, 421.
34. *Ibid.*, XI, 56, 497-98; XII, 23, 54.
35. Quoted in Rankin, pp. 175-76.
36. Wildes, p. 232.
37. Records of the General Assembly, Commonwealth of Pennsylvania, House of Representatives File, Pensions, Revolutionary War, Session of November 19, 1828.
38. Wildes, p. 232.

39. *Rev.* E. B. Hillard, *The Last Men of the Revolution* (Barre, Massachusetts: Barre Publishers, 1968), p. 71.

40. Chidsey, pp. 98-99.

41. Waldo, pp. 314-15.

42. Fitzpatrick, X, 365.

43. *Ibid.*, XI, 237-38; 285 note 75.

44. *Ibid.*, XI, 412.

45. *Ibid.*, XII, 30-31.

46. Ford, XI, 560-61.

47. Fitzpatrick, XII, 69.

48. *Ibid.*, X, 189, 215, 247-48.

49. *Ibid.*, X, 448-49; XI, 87, 126.

50. *Ibid.*, X, 211, 285, 449, 460-61; XI, 87, 229-30.

51. *Ibid.*, X, 269-30.

52. Waldo, pp. 314-15.

53. Fitzpatrick, X, 477; XI, 211.

54. *Ibid.*, XI, 286, 327.

55. *Ibid.*, XI, 139, 285.

56. *Ibid.*, X, 377.

57. Paul A. W. Wallace, *The Muhlenbergs of Pennsylvania* (Philadelphia: University of Pennsylvania Press, 1950), p. 170.

58. Fitzpatrick, X, 208, 490-91; XI, 19, 88, 173.

59. Wallace, pp. 170-71.

60. Fitzpatrick, XI, 233-34.

61. *Ibid.*, X, 450, 461-62, 485; XI, 234.

62. *Ibid.*, X, 303; XI, 15-18, 134-35; XII, 11, 45.

63. *Ibid.*, XI, 63-64, 66, 134-35; XII, 459.

64. Waldo, p. 308.

65. Fitzpatrick, XI, 485.

66. *Ibid.*, XI, 127-28, 224.

67. *Ibid.*, X, 238.

68. *Ibid.*, XI, 155.

69. Doyle, p. 86.

70. Fitzpatrick, XI, 252.

71. Greene, II, 84.

72. Reed, *Valley Forge,* p. 39.

73. McMichael, p. 216.

74. Fitzpatrick, XI, 21.

75. James Thatcher, *The Military Journal of the American Revolution* (New York: The New York Times and Arno Press, 1969), p. 146.

76. Greene, I, 565-66.

77. Fitzpatrick, X, 447.

78. Quoted in Bruce Lancaster, *From Lexington to Liberty* (Garden City, New York: Doubleday & Company, Inc., 1955), p. 337.

79. Chidsey, p. 120.

80. Ellet, II, 271.

81. Brooks, pp. 117-18.

82. Greene, II, 79.

83. Fisher, p. 9.

84. Greene, II, 74 note 1.

85. Hillard, pp. 71-72.

86. Wildes, p. 231.

87. Ewing, quoted in Stoudt, p. 233.

88. Stoudt, p. 280.

89. Ewing, quoted in Stoudt, p. 266.
90. Freeman, IV, 572 note 39.
91. Doyle, p. 86.
92. Fitzpatrick, X, 290.
93. *Ibid.*, XI, 267-68.
94. Chidsey, p. 110.
95. Brooks, p. 115.
96. Fitzpatrick, X, 167-68.
97. *Ibid.*, XI, 9.
98. Waldo, pp. 312-13.
99. McMichael, p. 217.
100. Freeman, IV, 550.
101. Fitzpatrick, X, 29.
102. Quoted in Freeman, IV, 590-91.
103. Fitzpatrick, X, 249.
104. *Ibid.*, X, 236-37.
105. *Ibid.*, X, 263-64.
106. *Ibid.*, X, 437-41.
107. *Ibid.*, X, 508.
108. Freeman, IV, 604.
109. Fitzpatrick, X, 529.
110. *Ibid.*, XI, 343, 393-94.
111. A. E. Zucker, *General De Kalb, Lafayette's Mentor* (Chapel Hill: University of North Carolina Press, 1966) , p. 179.

VI. HIGHLIGHTS AND SPECIAL EVENTS

1. Waldo, pp. 310-11, 315.
2. Fitzpatrick, X, 291.
3. McMichael, p. 216.
4. Waldo, p. 315.
5. Reed, *Valley Forge,* p. 27.
6. Fitzpatrick, X, 322.
7. Ford, X, 39-41.
8. Fitzpatrick, X, 362 note 27.
9. Ford, X, 41.
10. Reed, *Valley Forge,* p. 29.
11. Fitzpatrick, XI, 230.
12. *Ibid.*, X, 432-33.
13. *Ibid.*, XI, 113 and note 78
14. Theodore W. Bean, *Washington at Valley Forge* (Norristown: Charles P. Schreiner, 1876) , p. 36; Wildes, pp. 224-25.
15. Fisher, p. 7.
16. Elias Boudinot, *Journal or Historical Recollections of American Events During the Revolutionary War* (Philadelphia: Frederick Bourquin, 1894) , p. 78.
17. Ewing, quoted in Fitzpatrick, XI, 342 note 70.
18. Ewing, p. 48.
19. Fitzpatrick, XI, 354-55.
20. Ewing, pp. 48-49.
21. McMichael, p. 217.
22. Quoted in North Callahan, *Daniel Morgan, Ranger of the Revolution* (New York: Holt, Rinehart and Winston, 1961) , pp. 158-59.
23. Laurens, p. 169.
24. Fisher, pp. 7-8.

25. Ewing, p. 49.
26. Laurens, pp. 169-70.
27. Reed, *Valley Forge*, pp. 53-54.
28. Fitzpatrick, XI, 345.
29. Ford, X, 114-15.
30. Fitzpatrick, XI, 360-62.
31. *Ibid.*, XI, 374, 410-11 and note 78, 472.
32. Martin, pp. 118-19.
33. Gottschalk, p. 190.
34. Martin, p. 121.
35. Fisher, p. 8.
36. Martin, pp. 120-21.
37. Fisher, p. 8.
38. Fitzpatrick, XI, 443.

Appendix I

ORGANIZATIONS AT VALLEY FORGE, 1777-1778

I. *Continental Infantry Regiments*

Regiment	Brigade Commander
1st Connecticut[1]	Brig. Gen. Jedediah Huntington
2d Connecticut	Brig. Gen. Jedediah Huntington
4th Connecticut	Brig. Gen. James Varnum
5th Connecticut	Brig. Gen. Jedediah Huntington
7th Connecticut	Brig. Gen. Jedediah Huntington
8th Connecticut	Brig. Gen. James Varnum
1st Massachusetts	Brig. Gen. John Glover
2d Massachusetts	Brig. Gen. Ebenezer Learned
4th Massachusetts	Brig. Gen. John Glover
8th Massachusetts	Brig. Gen. Ebenezer Learned
9th Massachusetts	Brig. Gen. Ebenezer Learned
10th Massachusetts	Brig. Gen. John Paterson
11th Massachusetts	Brig. Gen. John Paterson
12th Massachusetts	Brig. Gen. John Paterson
13th Massachusetts	Brig. Gen. John Glover
14th Massachusetts	Brig. Gen. John Paterson
15th Massachusetts	Brig. Gen. John Glover
1st New Hampshire	Brig. Gen. Enoch Poor
2d New Hampshire	Brig. Gen. Enoch Poor
3d New Hampshire	Brig. Gen. Enoch Poor
1st New Jersey	Brig. Gen. William Maxwell
2d New Jersey	Brig. Gen. William Maxwell
3d New Jersey	Brig. Gen. William Maxwell
4th New Jersey[2]	Brig. Gen. William Maxwell
2d New York	Brig. Gen. Enoch Poor
4th New York	Brig. Gen. Enoch Poor
1st North Carolina	Brig. Gen. Lachlan McIntosh
2d North Carolina	Brig. Gen. Lachlan McIntosh
3d North Carolina	Brig. Gen. Lachlan McIntosh
4th North Carolina[3]	Brig. Gen. Lachlan McIntosh
5th North Carolina[3]	Brig. Gen. Lachlan McIntosh
6th North Carolina[3]	Brig. Gen. Lachlan McIntosh
7th North Carolina[4]	Brig. Gen. Lachlan McIntosh
8th North Carolina[4]	Brig. Gen. Lachlan McIntosh
9th North Carolina[4]	Brig. Gen. Lachlan McIntosh

[1] Although not included in the standard lists of regiments at Valley Forge, this regiment, or at least substantial elements of it, seems clearly to have been present at the encampment, as documented by the diary of its surgeon, Dr. Albigence Waldo. It is shown as part of Huntington's Brigade as of October, 1777, and as of the autumn of 1778, so presumably it would have been in that brigade during the months between.

[2] Personnel absorbed by 1st, 2d, and 3d New Jersey regiments, July 1, 1778.

[3] Personnel absorbed by 1st, 2d, and 3d North Carolina regiments, May 29, 1778.

[4] Disbanded, May 27, 1778.

Regiment	*Brigade Commander*
10th North Carolina[5]	Brig. Gen. Lachlan McIntosh
1st Pennsylvania	Col. Thomas Hartley (acting)
2d Pennsylvania	Col. Thomas Hartley (acting)
3d Pennsylvania	Brig. Gen. Thomas Conway[6]
4th Pennsylvania	Lt. Col. William Butler (acting)
5th Pennsylvania	Lt. Col. William Butler (acting)
6th Pennsylvania	Brig. Gen. Thomas Conway
7th Pennsylvania	Col. Thomas Hartley (acting)
8th Pennsylvania[7]	Lt. Col. William Butler (acting)
9th Pennsylvania	Brig. Gen. Thomas Conway
10th Pennsylvania	Col. Thomas Hartley (acting)
11th Pennsylvania[8]	Lt. Col. William Butler (acting)
12th Pennsylvania[9]	Brig. Gen. Thomas Conway
13th Pennsylvania[10]	Brig. Gen. George Weedon
1st Rhode Island	Brig. Gen. James Varnum
2d Rhode Island	Brig. Gen. James Varnum
1st Virginia	Brig. Gen. Peter Muhlenberg
2d Virginia	Brig. Gen. George Weedon
3d Virginia	Brig. Gen. George Weedon
4th Virginia[11]	Brig. Gen. George Weedon
5th Virginia[12]	Brig. Gen. Peter Muhlenberg
6th Virginia[13]	Brig. Gen. Peter Muhlenberg
7th Virginia[14]	Brig. Gen. William Woodford
8th Virginia[15]	Brig. Gen. Charles Scott
9th Virginia[16]	Brig. Gen. Peter Muhlenberg
10th Virginia[17]	Brig. Gen. George Weedon
11th Virginia[18]	Brig. Gen. William Woodford
12th Virginia[19]	Brig. Gen. Charles Scott
13th Virginia[20]	Brig. Gen. Peter Muhlenberg

---

[5] Recruited late 1777, arrived at Valley Forge by spring, 1778.

[6] Conway had been promoted major general and nominally appointed Inspector General, and left Valley Forge on December 31, 1777. This brigade, however, was invariably called "Conway's" or "late Conway's." Available records do not indicate who was its acting commander, if one was in fact named. Of the commanders of its component regiments, the senior colonel who could have been present for duty was Oliver Spencer, of Spencer's "Additional" Continental Regiment.

[7] Reassigned to Fort Pitt, March 8, 1778.

[8] Absorbed by 10th Pennsylvania, July 1, 1778.

[9] Absorbed by 3d Pennsylvania, July 1, 1778.

[10] Absorbed by 2d Pennsylvania, July 1, 1778.

[11] Absorbed by 3d Virginia, May 12, 1780.

[12] Absorbed by 3d Virginia. September 14, 1778.

[13] Absorbed by 2d Virginia, September 14, 1778.

[14] Redesignated as 5th Virginia, September 14, 1778.

[15] Absorbed by 4th Virginia, September 14, 1778.

[16] Only fragments of this regiment were at Valley Forge, as most of its members had been captured at the Battle of Germantown on October 4, 1777.

[17] Redesignated as 6th Virginia, September 14, 1778.

[18] Redesignated as 7th Virginia, September 14, 1778.

[19] Redesignated as 8th Virginia, September 14, 1778.

[20] Redesignated as 9th Virginia, September 14, 1778.

Regiment	*Brigade Commander*
14th Virginia[21]	Brig. Gen. George Weedon
The German Regiment[22]	Brig. Gen. Peter Muhlenberg
Grayson's "Additional" Continental Regiment[23]	Brig. Gen. Charles Scott
Hartley's "Additional" Continental Regiment[24]	Col. Thomas Hartley (acting)
Henley's "Additional" Continental Regiment[25]	Unassigned
Jackson's "Additional" Continental Regiment[26]	Unassigned
Malcom's "Additional" Continental Regiment[27]	Brig. Gen. Thomas Conway
Patton's "Additional" Continental Regiment[28]	Brig. Gen. Charles Scott
Spencer's "Additional" Continental Regiment[29]	Brig. Gen. Thomas Conway

II. State Infantry Regiment

1st Virginia State Regiment[30]	Brig. Gen. Peter Muhlenberg

III. Continental Artillery Regiments

1st Continental Artillery (elements)
2d Continental Artillery (elements)
3d Continental Artillery
4th Continental Artillery

IV. Continental Light Dragoons [31]

1st Continental Light Dragoons
2d Continental Light Dragoons
3d Continental Light Dragoons
4th Continental Light Dragoons

---

[21] Redesignated as 10th Virginia, September 14, 1778.

[22] With four of its companies raised in Pennsylvania and the other four in Maryland, this organization was credited to the Pennsylvania Line until February 26, 1778, when it was transferred to the Maryland Line and officially designated (but seldom referred to) as the 8th Maryland Continental Regiment.

[23] Absorbed by Gist's Ranger Corps, January 1, 1779.

[24] Consolidated with Patton's "Additional" Continental Regiment, January 13, 1779, to form the "New" 11th Pennsylvania.

[25] Consolidated with Jackson's "Additional" Continental Regiment, April 22, 1779.

[26] Redesignated as 16th Massachusetts, July 18, 1780.

[27] Absorbed by Spencer's "Additional" Continental Regiment, April 22, 1779.

[28] Consolidated with Hartley's "Additional" Continental Regiment, January 13, 1779, to form the "New" 11th Pennsylvania.

[29] Generally but unofficially called the 5th New Jersey Regiment.

[30] Reassigned from its State defense mission to replace the decimated 9th Virginia at Valley Forge.

[31] Shortly after arriving at Valley Forge, the bulk of the Light Dragoon regiments were reassigned to the vicinity of Trenton, N. J., to reduce the demand for forage in the Valley Forge area. Elements of at least the 1st Light Dragoons, however, remained at Valley Forge.

V. Miscellaneous Regiments

Regiment of Artillery Artificers (less detachments)
15th Virginia Continental Infantry[82]

VI. Brigade Commanders

Lt. Col. William Butler (acting commander, 2d Pennsylvania Brigade)
Brig. Gen. Thomas Conway (see note 6)
Brig. Gen. John Glover
Col. Thomas Hartley (acting commander, 1st Pennsylvania Brigade)
Brig. Gen. Jedediah Huntington
Brig. Gen. Henry Knox (Artillery Brigade)
Brig. Gen. Ebenezer Learned
Brig. Gen. Lachlan McIntosh
Brig. Gen. William Maxwell
Brig. Gen. Peter Muhlenberg
Brig. Gen. John Paterson
Brig. Gen. Enoch Poor
Brig. Gen. Charles Scott
Brig. Gen. James Varnum
Brig. Gen. George Weedon
Brig. Gen. William Woodford

VII. Divisional Organization

Clearly, there was no comprehensive attempt to establish a divisional
structure at Valley Forge, and such incomplete structure as did exist
does not seem to have been consistently maintained, due to the turn-
over in major generals apart from any other considerations.

The following major generals were present for varying periods of
time during the encampment:

Johan De Kalb (absent from late January to mid-March for the
Canadian "irruption." Learned's and Paterson's brigades appear
to have comprised a division under his part-time command).

Nathanael Greene (commanded a division consisting of Muhlenberg's and Weedon's brigades).

Marquis de Lafayette (absent from late January to mid-March for
the Canadian "irruption").

Charles Lee (arrived at Valley Forge only in April, 1778).

Friedrich von Steuben (Inspector General—no command assignment).

Lord Stirling (chiefly occupied in supervising artificer and engineer
activities).

---

[82] The possibility exists that this regiment was at Valley Forge as part of Brig.
Gen. William Woodford's brigade. Evidence, however, is inconclusive. This regiment was redesignated as the 11th Virginia, September 14, 1778.

John Sullivan (McIntosh's and Maxwell's brigades were nominally in a division under Sullivan, but Sullivan was transferred from Valley Forge to duties elsewhere in February, 1778).

In addition to the divisions mentioned above, the two Pennsylvania brigades appear to have been considered to comprise a division, commanded by Brig. Gen. Anthony Wayne.

Appendix II

BATTALION (REGIMENTAL) MANNING LEVELS
ADOPTED MAY 27, 1778

	Infantry	Artillery	Dragoons
Colonel	1	1	1
Lieutenant Colonel	1	1	1
Major	1	1	1
Captain	6	12	6
Captain-Lieutenant	1	12	–
First Lieutenant	–	12	–
Lieutenant	8	–	12
Second Lieutenant	–	36	–
Ensign	9	–	–
Cornet	–	–	6
Riding Master	–	–	1
Surgeon	1	1	1
Surgeon's Mate	1	1	1
Sadler	–	–	1
Farrier	–	–	6
Quartermaster Sergeant	1	1	6
Sergeant Major	1	1	–
Sergeant	27	72	12
Drum Major	1	1	–
Fife Major	1	1	–
Trumpet Major	–	–	1
Drummer and Fifer	18	24	–
Trumpeter	–	–	6
Bombardier	–	72	–
Corporal	27	72	30
Gunner	–	72	–
Matross	–	336	–
Private	477	–	–
Dragoon	–	–	324
TOTALS	573	729	416

Appendix III

MONTHLY PAY RATES APPROVED MAY 27, 1778

	Infantry	Artillery	Dragoons
Colonel	$75	$100	$93 3/4
Lieutenant Colonel	60	75	75
Major	50	62 1/2	60
Captain	40	50	50
Captain-Lieutenant	26 2/3	33 1/3	–
First Lieutenant	–	33 1/3	
Lieutenant	26 2/3	–	33 1/3
Second Lieutenant	–	33 1/3	–
Ensign	20	–	–
Cornet	–	–	26 2/3
Riding Master	–	–	33 1/3
Surgeon	60	75	60
Surgeon's Mate	40	50	40
Sadler	–	–	10
Farrier	–	–	10
Sergeant Major	10	11 23/90	–
Quartermaster Sergeant	10	11 23/90	15
Sergeant	10	10	15
Drum Major	9	10 38/90	–
Fife Major	9	10 38/90	–
Trumpet Major	–	–	11
Drummer and Fifer	7 1/3	8 2/3	–
Trumpeter	–	–	10
Bombardier	–	9	–
Corporal	7 1/3	9	10
Gunner	–	8 2/3	–
Matross	–	8 1/3	–
Private	6 2/3	–	–
Dragoon	–	–	8 1/3

Bibliography

PRIMARY SOURCES: BOOKS

BOUDINOT, ELIAS. *Journal or Historical Recollections of American Events During the Revolutionary War*. Philadelphia: Frederick Bourquin, 1894.

EWING, GEORGE. *The Military Journal of George Ewing, A Soldier of Valley Forge.* New York: Privately Printed, 1928.

FISHER, ELIJAH. *Elijah Fisher's Journal While in the War for Independence, and Continued Two Years After He Came to Maine, 1775-1784.* Augusta, Me.: Press of Badger and Manley, 1880.

FITZPATRICK, JOHN C. (ed.). *The Writings of George Washington From the Original Manuscript Sources, 1744-1799.* Volumes X-XII. Washington: U. S. Government Printing Office, 1933.

FORD, WILLIAM CHAUNCEY (ed.). *Journals of the Continental Congress.* Volume X. Washington: Government Printing Office, 1908.

LAURENS, JOHN. *The Army Correspondence of Colonel John Laurens in the Years 1777-8.* New York: Arno Press, Inc., 1969.

MARTIN, JOSEPH PLUMB. *Private Yankee Doodle, Being a Narrative of Some of the Adventures, Dangers and Sufferings of a Revolutionary Soldier.* Edited by George F. Scheer. Boston, Toronto: Little, Brown and Company, 1962.

MUHLENBERG, HENRY MELCHIOR. *The Journals of Henry Melchior Muhlenberg.* Volume III. Philadelphia: The Muhlenberg Press, 1958.

Records of the General Assembly, Commonwealth of Pennsylvania, House of Representatives File, Pensions, Revolutionary War, Session of November 19, 1828.

THATCHER, JAMES. *The Military Journal of the American Revolution.* New York: The New York Times and Arno Press, 1969.

WEEDON, GEORGE. *Valley Forge Orderly Book.* New York: Dodd, Mead and Company, 1902.

PRIMARY SOURCES: PERIODICALS

CLARK, JOSEPH. "Diary," *Proceedings of the New Jersey Historical Society,* Volume VII.

JORDAN, JOHN W. (ed.). "Orderly Book of the Second Pennsylvania Continental Line Col. Henry Bicker. At Valley Forge, March 29-May 27, 1778," *Pennsylvania Magazine of History and Biography,* Volumes XXXV-XXXVI.

MCMICHAEL, LIEUTENANT JAMES. "Diary, 1776-1778," *Pennsylvania Archives,* Second Series, Volume XV.

MONTRÉSOR, CAPTAIN JOHN. "Journal, July 1, 1777 to July 1, 1778." Edited by G. D. Scull. *Pennsylvania Magazine of History and Biography,* Volumes V-VI.

"Orderly Book of General Edward Hand, Valley Forge, January, 1778," *Pennsylvania Magazine of History and Biography,* Volume XLI.

PAINE, THOMAS. "Military Operations Near Philadelphia in the Campaign of 1777-1778. Described in a Letter from Thomas Paine to Dr. Franklin," *Pennsylvania Magazine of History and Biography.* Volume II.

WALDO, DR. ALBIGENCE. "Valley Forge, 1777-1778. Diary of Surgeon Albigence Waldo of the Connecticut Line," *Pennsylvania Magazine of History and Biography,* Volume XXI.

SECONDARY SOURCES: BOOKS

BEAN, THEODORE W. *Washington at Valley Forge.* Norristown: Charles P. Schreiner, 1876.

BILL, HOYT. *Valley Forge.* New York: Harper & Brothers, 1952.

BINING, ARTHUR CECIL. *Pennsylvania Iron Manufacture in the Eighteenth Century.* Harrisburg: Pennsylvania Historical Commission, 1938.

BLAINE, HARRY S. *Who Stole the Shoes at Valley Forge? A Tragedy and Vindication.* Toledo, Ohio, 1966.

BLUMENTHAL, WALTER HART. *Women Camp Followers of the American Revolution.* Philadelphia: George S. McManus Company, 1952.

BOLTON, CHARLES KNOWLES. *The Private Soldier Under Washington.* New York: Charles Scribner's Sons, 1902.

BOWMAN, ALLAN. *The Morale of the American Revolutionary Army.* Washington: American Council on Public Affairs, 1943.

BOYD, THOMAS. *Mad Anthony Wayne.* New York: Charles Scribner's Sons, 1929.

BROOKS, NOAH. *Henry Knox.* New York: G. P. Putnam's Sons, 1900.

BUSCH, NOEL F. *Winter Quarters.* New York: Liveright, 1974.

CALLAHAN, NORTH. *Daniel Morgan, Ranger of the Revolution.* New York: Holt, Rinehart and Winston, 1961.

CHIDSEY, DONALD BARR. *Valley Forge.* New York: Crown Publishers, Inc., 1956, 1966.

COLONIAL DAMES OF AMERICA. *Forges and Furnaces in the Province of Pennsylvania.* Philadelphia: Printed for the Society, 1914.

DOYLE, JOSEPH B. *Frederick William von Steuben and The American Revolution.* New York: Burt Franklin, 1913, 1970.

DUNCAN, LOUIS C. *Medical Men in the American Revolution 1775-1783.* Carlisle Barracks, Pennsylvania: Medical Field Service School, 1931.

ELLET, ELIZABETH F. *Women of the American Revolution.* Philadelphia: George W. Jacobs & Co., 1900. 2 Volumes.

FORD, WORTHINGTON CHAUNCEY (ed.). *Defences of Philadelphia in 1777.* New York: Da Capo, 1971.

FREEMAN, DOUGLAS SOUTHALL. *George Washington: A Biography.* Volume IV. New York: Charles Scribner's Sons, 1951.

GANOE, WILLIAM ADDLEMAN. *The History of the United States Army.* New York: D. Appleton-Century Company, Inc., 1942.

GOTTSCHALK, LOUIS. *Lafayette Joins the American Army.* Chicago: University of Chicago Press, 1937.

GREENE, FRANCIS VINTON. *General Greene.* New York: D. Appleton and Company, 1893.

GREENE, GEORGE WASHINGTON. *The Life of Nathanael Greene.* New York: Hurd and Houghton, 1871. 3 Volumes.

HILLARD, REV. E. B. *The Last Men of the Revolution.* Edited by Wendell D. Garrett. Barre, Massachusetts: Barre Publishers, 1968.

KITE, ELIZABETH S. *Brigadier-General Louis Lebèque Duportail.* Baltimore: The Johns Hopkins Press, 1933.

LANCASTER, BRUCE. *From Lexington to Liberty.* Garden City, New York: Doubleday & Company, Inc., 1955.

McDOWELL, BART. *The Revolutionary War.* Washington: The National Geographic Society, 1967.

MONTROSS, LYNN. *Rag, Tag and Bobtail.* New York: Harper & Brothers Publishers, 1952.

NOLAN, J. BENNETT. *Lafayette in America Day by Day.* Baltimore, The Johns Hopkins Press, 1934.

PALMER, JOHN MCAULEY. *General von Steuben.* New Haven: Yale University Press, 1937.

QUARLES, BENJAMIN. *The Negro in the American Revolution.* Chapel Hill: University of North Carolina Press, 1961.

RANKIN, HUGH F. *The American Revolution.* New York: G. P. Putnam's Sons, 1964.

REED, JOHN F. *Campaign to Valley Forge, July 1, 1777-December 19, 1777.* Philadelphia: University of Pennsylvania Press, 1965.

————. *Valley Forge, Crucible of Victory.* Monmouth Beach, New Jersey: Philip Freneau Press, 1969.

ROBERTS, OCTAVIA. *With Lafayette in America.* Boston: Houghton Mifflin Company, 1919.

ROSSMAN, KENNETH R. *Thomas Mifflin and the Politics of the American Revolution.* Chapel Hill: University of North Carolina Press, 1952.

SMITH, SAMUEL STELLE. *The Battle of Monmouth.* Monmouth Beach, New Jersey: Philip Freneau Press, 1964.

————. *Fight for the Delaware 1777.* Monmouth Beach, New Jersey: Philip Freneau Press, 1970.

STOUDT, JOHN JOSEPH. *Ordeal at Valley Forge.* Philadelphia: University of Pennsylvania Press, 1963.

STRYKER, WILLIAM S. *The Battle of Monmouth.* Princeton: Princeton University Press, 1927.

TAYLOR, FRANK H. *Valley Forge: A Chronicle of American Heroism.* Philadelphia: James W. Nagle, Publisher, 1905.

THOMPSON, RAY. *Washington at Germantown.* Fort Washington, Pennsylvania: The Bicentennial Press, 1971.

————. *Washington at Whitemarsh.* Fort Washington, Pennsylvania: The Bicentennial Press, n. d.

VALENTINE, ALAN. *Lord Stirling.* New York: Oxford University Press, 1969.

WALLACE, PAUL A. W. *The Muhlenbergs of Pennsylvania.* Philadelphia: University of Pennsylvania Press, 1950.

WHEELER, RICHARD. *Voices of 1776.* New York: Thomas Y. Crowell Company, 1972.

WILDES, HARRY EMERSON. *Anthony Wayne.* New York: Harcourt Brace and Company, 1941.

————. *Valley Forge.* New York: The Macmillan Company, 1938.

ZUCKER, A. E. *General De Kalb, Lafayette's Mentor.* Chapel Hill: University of North Carolina Press, 1966.

SECONDARY SOURCES: PERIODICALS

ATKINSON, PAUL G., JR. "The System of Military Discipline and Justice in the Continental Army: August 1777-June 1778," *The Picket Post,* Winter, 1972-1973.

BRENNEMAN, GLORIA E. "The Conway Cabal: Myth or Reality," *Pennsylvania History,* Volume XL.

JENKINS, HOWARD M. "The Old Iron Forge—'Valley Forge,'" *Pennsylvania Magazine of History and Biography,* Volume XVII.

Index

Abatis, 50-51
Adams, John, 66
Addison, Joseph, 96
Albany, N. Y., 4, 106
Alexander, William (see Stirling, Maj. Gen. Lord William)
Allentown, Pa., 9
Alliance with France, 77, 96, 103-104, 109-10
American Revolution, iii, 2, 96, 100, 115-16
Ammunition, 54-56, 59, 67
Amusements (see also Athletics), 95-96, 98, 108
Armory Department, 55
Armstrong, Maj. Gen. John, 9-10, 55
Army, British, 3-6, 8-13, 17, 26, 32, 34-35, 40, 51, 57-58, 63, 65-66, 70, 75, 78, 81, 100, 105-106, 111-12, 115
Army, Continental, iii-iv, 3-6, 8-9, 11, 15, 17, 21, 27-28, 30-31, 33-35, 37, 39, 44-45, 47, 52, 55, 57-58, 62, 65, 75, 78-80, 82, 85, 88, 93-94, 97, 102, 106, 113, 116
Army, Hessian, 4-5, 46, 78
Arnold, Benedict, 95
Articles of War, 66-68
Artificers (see Engineers)
Artillery (see also individual regiments), 4, 13, 26, 30, 50-51, 53-55, 71, 77, 79, 82, 88, 92-93, 96, 109
Artillery Artificer Regiment, 130
Athletics, 82-83, 96
Aubrey, William, 1

Baden, 58
"Bakehouse," 23, 96
Baptist Road, 49-50
Barren Hill, 77, 111-13
"Base" (see Rounders)
Baseball (see Rounders)
Baylies, Maj. Hadijah, 72
Bayonet, 54, 61
Bethlehem, Pa., 13, 41, 47
Biddle, Col. Clement, 95
Biddle, Rebecca (Mrs. Clement), 95
Bloom, John, 75
Board of War, 55, 68, 97, 100, 103, 106
Borre, Brig. Gen. Prud'Homme de, 6
Boston, Mass., 3, 22, 28, 100
Boudinot, Elias, 95, 108
Bowdoin, James, 78
Bowling, 83
Brandywine, Battle of, 3, 5-6, 64, 71, 92, 99
Brandywine Creek, 5

Bride, Pvt. Jeremiah, 73
Bristol, Pa., 11
Bucks County, Pa., 110
Bunker Hill, Battle of, 51, 78
Burgoyne, Gen. John, 4-5, 10-11, 116
Burris, Pvt. Samuel, 73
Butler, Thomas, 74
Butler, Lt. Col. William, 128, 130

Cadwalader, Brig. Gen. John, 81
Cameron, Pvt., 74
Canada, 3-4, 106, 130
Capital punishment, 67-70
Carbines, 53-54
Carlisle, Pa., 55
Carroll, Charles, 106
Casualties, Battle, iii, 8, 39-40, 52, 110
Cato, 96
Cavalry, American (see also individual regiments), 6, 13, 25-26, 28, 53-55, 79, 88, 105, 111-12
Cavalry, British, 105, 110, 113, 129 & note 31
Chadd's Ford, Pa., 5
Chaplains, 11, 15, 82-83, 109
Charleston, S. C., 3
Chesapeake Bay, 4-5
Chester, Pa., 6
Chester Springs, Pa. (see Yellow Springs)
Chester Valley, 8
Chew House (see Cliveden)
Civilians, 27, 31-32, 34-35, 65, 69, 74-75, 83, 96, 99-100, 112
Clime, Pvt. John, 74
Clinton, Gov. George, 80
Clinton, Gen. Sir Henry, 51
Cliveden, 10
Clothing (see also Shoes), 11, 18, 21, 26-31, 33, 35, 38-39, 41, 43, 45, 47
Committee on Conference, 22, 26, 31, 34-35, 40, 42, 55, 68, 77, 80, 85, 102, 105-106
Congress, Second Continental, iv, 3, 8-9, 13, 17, 22, 26, 28-31, 33-35, 46, 53, 58, 62, 65-67, 74, 77, 79, 83, 86-88, 90-92, 97, 100-103, 105-106, 110, 113
Connecticut troops (see also individual regiments), 17, 28, 52, 77
Conner, Pvt. John, 74
Conolly, Matross Edward, 73-74
Conshohocken, Pa. (see Matson's Ford)
Conway, Maj. Gen. Thomas, 51, 58-59, 62, 100-103, 128 & note 6, 130
"Conway Cabal," 58-59, 100-103, 129

139